SCIENTIFIC SCHOOLS.

PART I. FRANCE.

THE POLYTECHNIC SCHOOL AT PARIS.

[Republished from Barnard's American Journal of Education.]

Military Publications.

Published by J. B. LIPPINCOTT & CO., Philadelphia.

Will be forwarded by mail, postpaid, on receipt of the price by the Publishers.

Surgery of War. Commentaries on the Surgery of the War in Portugal, Spain, France, the Netherlands, and the Crimea. By G. J. GUTHRIE, F. R. S. One vol. 12mo. $2.25.

Surgery of the Crimean War. With Remarks on the Treatment of Gunshot Wounds. By G. H. B. MACLEOD, M D., F.R.C.S. One vol. 12mo. $1.50.

The Art of War. By BARON DE JOMINI, General and Aid-de-Camp of the Emperor of Russia. A new Edition, with Appendices and Maps. One vol. demi 8vo. $1.50.

Marmont's Military Institutions. Translated, with Notes, by Capt. HENRY COPPEE, U S.A. One vol. 12mo.

United States Cavalry Tactics. Cavalry Tactics; or, Regulations for the Instruction, Formations, and Movements of Cavalry. Authorized and adopted by the Secretary of War, Nov. 1, 1861. By PHILIP ST. GEORGE COOKE, Brig-Gen. U. S. A. In two vols. 18mo. Price 1.50.

Revised Army Regulations. By authority of the President of the United States and the Secretary of War. One vol 8vo. $1.75.

Field Artillery Instruction. Prepared by a Board of Artillery Officers. One volume, 8vo. $2.50.

Hardee's Tactics. Rifle and Light Infantry Tactics, for the Exercise and Manœuvres of Troops. Prepared under the direction of the War Department. Two volumes complete. $1.50.

United States Infantry Tactics. Prepared under the direction of the War Department. One vol. $1.25.

Instructions for Outpost and Patrol Duty, and the Skirmish Drill for Mounted Troops. Authorized and adopted by the Secretary of War, Sept. 2, 1861. 25 cts.

Manual for Courts Martial, with Complete Forms of Proceedings. By Captain HENRY COPPEE, late Instructor at the U. S. Military Academy. 18mo.

Manual of Target Practice, for the U. States Army. By Major GEO. L. WILLARD, U.S.A. 18mo.

Summary of the Art of War. By EMIL SCHALK, illustrated. 12mo. $1.50.

School of the Brigade and Evolutions of the Line. A Sequel to the U. S. Infantry Tactics. By Col. WM. W. DUFFIELD. 18mo.

The Armies of Europe. Comprising descriptions in detail of the Military Systems of England, France, Russia, Prussia, Austria, and Sardinia. By GEORGE B. MCCLELLAN, Major-General U.S.A. 1 vol 8vo. Illustrated with a fine steel Portrait and several hundred engravings. $3.50.

Regulations and Instructions for the Field Service of the United States Cavalry. By GEO. B. MCCLELLAN, Major-Gen. U.S.A. 12mo. Fully illustrated. $1.50.

Manual of Bayonet Exercises. Prepared for the use of the Army of the United States. By GEO. B. MCCLELLAN, Major-Gen. U.S.A. One vol. 12mo. $1.25.

European Cavalry, including details of the organization of the Cavalry Service among the principal nations of Europe. By GEO. B. MCCLELLAN, Major-Gen. U.S.A. 1 vol. 12mo. Fully illustrated. $1.25.

Cavalry Tactics. Published by order of the War Department. 3 vols, 18mo. $3.75.

Ordnance Manual. Prepared under the direction of the War Department. Third edition. One vol, demi 8vo. Fully illustrated with Engravings on Steel. $2.50.

Field Manual of Evolutions of the Line, arranged in a tabular form. Translated, with adaptation to the United States Service, from the latest French authorities, by Capt. HENRY COPPEE. 18mo. 50 cts.

The Field Manual of Battalion Drill. Containing all the movements and manœuvres in the School of the the Battalion, with the commands arranged in tabular forms. Translated from the French, with adaptation to the U. States Service, by Capt. HENRY COPPEE. 18mo. 50 cts.

Gunshot Wounds. A Treatise on Gunshot Wounds. By T. LONGMORE, Deputy Instructor of Hospitals, Professor of Military Surgery at Fort Pitt, Chatham. One vol. 12mo. 75 cts.

Soldier's Handy-Book. The Handy-Book for the U. S Soldier on coming into Service. Being a First Book or Introduction to the authorized U. States Infantry Tactics. 25 cts.

Military Encyclopædia. A comprehensive Encyclopædia of Military Science, Art, and History; containing a Complete Explanation of all Military Terms, with their Pronunciation, and Descriptions of the Principal Battles in the World's History. Fully illustrated. [In press.]

Military Schools and Education in all Countries.—Drawn from latest Official Documents. By HENRY BARNARD. France and Prussia. One volume. 8vo. $2 50.

Polytechnic School of France. One volume. 8vo. $1.00.

Calisthenic, Gymnastic and Military Exercises in Public Schools. Part one, 15 cents.

Military Schools and Education in the United States. One volume. 8vo. $1.50. [In press.]

PHYSICAL EDUCATION.

J. B. Lippincott & Co., Philadelphia, will issue a series of Papers, edited by Henry Barnard, LL. D., on Calisthenic, Gymnastic and Military Exercises, and Physical Education generally, in Schools public and private.

The following list embraces a portion of the subjects which will be discussed, but not the order in which they will be issued.

I. Thoughts on Physical Culture by various Authors, ancient and modern.

II. Health Movements for Home and School.

III. Calisthenic Exercises for Girls.

IV. Gymnastic Exercises for Boys.

V. The Industrial Element in Schools.

VI. The Military Element in Education, and the History and Place of Military Schools, in a System of Public Instruction.

VII. Military Exercises and Discipline in Schools, not specially Military.

VIII. Account of Juvenile Schools not specially Military, in which Military Discipline and Drill are introduced.

IX. The Military System, Cadet Corps and Target Shooting in Switzerland.

X. Manual for Cadet Corps in Schools.

XI. Military Gymnastics as practiced in France and Prussia.

XII. The French and English Schools of Musketry.

NOW READY.

Number 1. *Physical and Military Exercises in Public Schools.* By Major E. L. Molineux. Price 15 cts.

Number 2. *Health Movements for Home and School.* By Dr. Dio Lewis. Price 10 cents.

Number 3. *Switzerland—its Military System, Cadet Corps, and Target Festivals.* By Prof. Simonson. Price 10 cents.

THE following Papers on SCIENTIFIC SCHOOLS, in which the Principles of Science are taught with special reference to their Applications to the Arts of Peace and War in different countries, were prepared mostly from official documents or after personal visits by the writers, for publication in the AMERICAN JOURNAL OF EDUCATION. It is now proposed to bring them together in a volume, in the hope that this comprehensive survey of the entire field of European experience may impress the public mind with the number, character and influence of this class of schools, and at the same time furnish useful hints in the organization and instruction of similar schools in this country.

Before being gathered in a volume, the accounts will be issued in Parts—each Part being devoted to a particular country. PART I. will be an exception to this rule, and will be devoted exclusively to the Polytechnic School of France, the best school of the kind in the world.

HARTFORD, CONN. H. B.

CONTENTS.

INTRODUCTION.

FRANCE is distinguished among European nations for the number, variety and excellence of schools which provide for special professional education. Under the direction of the government, are not less than nine schools of law, at Paris, Aix, Caen, Dijon, Grenoble, Poitiers, Rennes, Strasbourg, and Toulouse; three schools of medicine, at Paris, Montpellier, and Strasbourg; three schools of pharmacy at the same places; six faculties of theology, and eighty-three grand seminaries of theology of the Catholic church, (one in almost every diocese,) two Protestant faculties and seminaries at Strasbourg and Montauban, and a Rabbinical school at Metz. In the different departments there are not less than eighty-three seminaries or normal schools for male and female teachers. Special provision is made for military and naval instruction in the celebrated Imperial school at Saint Cyr, for the training of infantry, artillery and cavalry officers; in the Imperial naval school at Brest, (upon the vessel *le Borda*,) for the education of officers of the government marine; and in the Imperial school of military medicine and pharmacy at Paris, for the education of army physicians.

Provision of the most liberal character is made for advanced scientific and literary education in the faculties of the *University*. The title "University" was formerly applied in France, as it still is in Germany to separate institutions of learning, of which there were many,—that of Paris, being the most celebrated. After the great revolution, Napoleon arranged all the departments of public instruction in the empire into one system, which was styled *the* University of France. This appellation, if not formally, is virtually dropped at present, but the "Faculties" of the university are still, and always have been spoken of much in the same way as in Germany and other countries.

Thus the system of public instruction in France, recognizes five distinct faculties; theology, law, medicine, physical and mathematical sciences and letters.

In the empire there are 16 faculties of science, sometimes associated with, and sometimes disconnected from the other faculties above named. They are established at Paris, Besancon, Bordeaux, Caen,

Clermont, Dijon, Grenoble, Lille, Lyon, Marseilles, Montpellier, Nancy, Poitiers, Rennes, Strasbourg and Toulouse.

The scientific faculty at Paris, in the Sorbonne, numbers eighteen professors, (besides five *agrégés**) among whom are many men of the highest distinction, Leverrier, Dumas, Milne-Edwards, &c.

The following are the present departments of instruction ;—physical astronomy; mathematical astronomy; higher algebra; higher geometry; differential and integral calculus; mechanics; physical and experimental mechanics; calculus of probabilities, and mathematical physics; general physics, (two professors;) chemistry, (two professors;) mineralogy; geology; botany; general physiology; zoölogy, anatomy, and physiology; anatomy, comparative physiology and zoölogy.

The other faculties of science are naturally less complete than that of Paris, and it is deemed enough to mention the number of professors, without specifying their departments. It is as follows: Besancon, six; Bordeaux, six; Caen, five; Clermont, four; Dijon, six; Grenoble, five; Lille, four; Lyon, seven; Marseilles, four; Montpellier, seven; Nancy, four; Poitiers, four; Rennes, six; Strasbourg, six; Toulouse, eight.

The faculties of letters in France are 16 in number, and are in the same towns with the faculties of science, except that there are two of the former at Aix and Douai, and none at Lille and Marseilles. At Paris, in the Sorbonne, twelve chairs are occupied by this faculty, namely; philosophy, history of philosophy, Greek literature, Latin eloquence, Latin poetry, French eloquence, French poetry, foreign literature, comparative grammar, ancient history, modern history, and geography. There are four honorary professors, Messrs. Guizot, Villemain, Cousin, and Boissonade, and twenty agreges. In the provincial towns, the number of professors in the faculty of Letters, is nearly the same as in that of the faculties of science.

There are four schools of a preparatory character, in which there are instructors both of Science and Letters at Angers, Mulhouse, Nantes and Rouen.

Subordinate to these faculties are the lyceums, 62 in number, and colleges, 245 in number, which are "secondary" in their rank, and hold nearly the same position in France, as the gymnasiums and real-schools in Germany. The limits of this article will not allow of their examination.

There is one college, however, which is an exception,—the Imperial College of France, which was founded in 1530. Although now

*The *agrégés* in France correspond nearly to the Privat Docenten in Germany.

nominally under the ministry of public instruction, it has always been an independent establishment, and was not even included in the university organization of the Emperor Napoleon. In this institution there are thirty-four readers and professors in the following departments:—astronomy, mathematics, general and mathematical physics, general and experimental physics, chemistry, medicine, natural history of inorganic bodies, natural history of organic bodies, comparative embryology, natural and statute law, history of legislation, political economy, history and morals, archæology, Hebrew, Chaldaic, and Syriac languages, Arabic language, Persian language, Turkish language, Chinese and Tartar-mandchou language and literature, Sanskrit language, Greek language and literature, Latin eloquence, Latin poetry, Greek and Latin philosophy, French language and literature in the middle ages, modern French language and literature, languages and literature of modern Europe, Slavic languages and literature.

Some of the professors here, are also professors at the Sorbonne. Many of their names are of the highest distinction for example. Michel Chevalier, Elie de Beaumont, Biot, Stanislas Julien, &c.

In this place may also be mentioned the lectures of the Museum of Natural History, at the celebrated Garden of Plants. Connected with this institution are professors devoted to the following departments of natural history and science; comparative physiology; comparative anatomy; anatomy, and natural history of man; zoölogy, (mammalia and birds;) zoölogy, (reptiles and fishes;) zoölogy, (insects, crustacea, and arachnides;) zoölogy, (Annelides, molluscs, and zoöphytes;) botany; cultivation; geology; mineralogy; palæontology; physics applied to natural history; organic chemistry; inorganic chemistry.

It thus appears that in sixteen faculties of science, the college of France, and the museum of natural history, instruction in pure science, of the most elevated order is provided, and that in sixteen faculties of letters, corresponding advantages are offered for literary pursuits.

But this is by no means all. The natural sciences, in their applications, are taught in a large number of central schools, established for the most part at Paris, and usually bearing the title "Imperial," as a recognition of the high estimation in which they are held by the government. In the provincial cities and towns, subordinate schools of science are found, of grades which correspond to the "Secondary," and "Primary" schools, ordinarily so called in the continental systems of public instruction. Many graduates of the higher Imperial schools become teachers in the lower schools, by means of which a practical knowledge of science is well diffused among all classes in society. Other graduates of the higher schools ultimately take the chief direction of mines, chemical and other manufacturing establishments, works of civil engineering, architectural undertakings. and immense landed estates, or they enter some administrative department of the government which demands a deep knowledge of science, for example, the mint, the inspection of drugs, foods, &c.; while the subordinate positions, either in industrial callings, or in these branches of civil service are filled by those whohave studied in the lower class of schools. There are also special schools of a Literary character.

From the institutions for instruction in pure science, and in the highest departments of literature, we accordingly pass to a consideration of those institutions in which the applications of science hold a prominent place, or literary pursuits are followed with some practical aim. Information mostly derived from official sources, will be given concerning all the more important, beginning with those of a literary character.

The following special schools of language and history are established by the French government.

1. *The Imperial School of Records*, (Ecole des Chartes,) at Paris. This institution, begun in 1821, and connected with the Imperial Library, prepares young men for the duties of librarians and keepers of public archives. Candidates for admission must be not less than 24 years old, and must have received the degree of *Bachelier ès Lettres.* The course of studies occupies three years, at the end of which those who have passed a successful examination, receive the diploma of *Archiviste paléographe.* This diploma gives the right to a salary of 600 francs for three years to six former pupils of the school. This right is lost by refusing to accept a position in the public employments open to the archivists, such as the duties of librarians, archive keepers, teachers in the *Ecole des Chartes*, &c. There are eight scholarships, (*bourses*,) open to the pupils of this school, the annual income of each being 600 francs. The pupils are charged with the publication of the *Documents inédits de l'histoire de France.*

There are seven professors in the school who instruct in the deciphering of manuscripts and documents, in geography and history, the use of seals, value of monies and measures, study of languages, archæology, &c., &c.

2. *School of living Oriental Languages.* This school, also connected with the Imperial Library, was founded in 1795, with a view to advancing the interests of the government service, military and civil, in Asia and Africa, and at the same time, to encouraging linguistic science. There are nine chairs, namely,—Arabic; Persian; Tur

kish; Armenian; modern Greek, and Greek Palæography; common Arabic; Hindoostani; Chinese; Malay, and Japanese.

3. *Course in Archaeology.* A course of instruction in Archaeology in connection with the cabinet of medals in the Imperial Library, was commenced in 1795, with a view to making known the monuments of art and the historical monuments of antiquity.

4. *French School at Athens, Greece.* The object of this school is to give young professors the means of perfecting themselves in the language, history and antiquities of Greece. The members of the school are named by the minister of public instruction, after a special examination in the Greek language, ancient and modern, the elements of palæography and archaeology, and the history and geography of Greece. They reside at Athens two years, (and may do so by special permission for a third year,) during which time they receive a special salary.

We now proceed to consider separately, the higher institutions for instruction in the applications of science. They vary of course in their character, rank, and requirements for admission. Some of them are under the direction of the ministry of public instruction, others under the ministry of agriculture, commerce, and public works, the ministry of the interior, and the ministry of war. As it is difficult to choose a proper order for their enumeration, that of the *Annuaire de l'Instruction Publique*, will here be followed.

1. *Imperial Schools of Agriculture* are established at Grignon, Grand-Jouan, and la Saulsaie, and St. Angean. Candidates for admission must be at least 17 years old, and must pass an examination in arithmetic, geometry, and physics, and in French orthography, and grammar. The course of studies lasts three years, at the end of which certificates of capacity are awarded.

In addition to these three high schools of agriculture, there are forty-nine of subordinate farm schools, (fermes-écoles,) situated in the different departments of the empire.

2. *Imperial Veterinary Schools* are located at Alfert, Lyon, and Toulouse. These schools are to train veterinary surgeons, for military and civil service. The candidates for admission must be between 17 and 25 years old, and the course of studies last four years.

3. *Imperial Schools of Arts and Trades* have been founded at Châlons sur Marne, since the year of the Republic; at Angers since 1811; and Aix since 1843. Pupils to be admitted must be between 15 and 17 years old; their instruction continues for three years, and is both theoretical and practical in its character. The scholars are fitted to be the heads of manufacturing establishments, foremen in

shops, &c., receiving a more practical education than in the following higher schools.

4. *The Central School of Arts and Manufactures* at Paris, was begun in 1829 as a private institution, intended to prepare civil engineers, directors of manufactories, professors of applied science, &c. It is now under government direction, and prepares its pupils in four specialties; chemistry, mechanics, metal working, and civil engineering. Candidates for admission must be at least 16 years old, and must pass a satisfactory examination in arithmetic, algebra, geometry, and designing. The complete course of instruction extends through three years. In the third year pupils may be examined for the diploma of civil engineer, and certificates of capacity may be awarded to those who excel only in some of the departments of study.

5. *The Imperial School of Mines*, at Paris, is designed to train government engineers, but pupils are received who do not intend to enter the public service. Candidates for entrance must be between 18 and 25 years of age, and must pass an examination in arithmetic, algebra, geometry, rectilinear trigonometry, theory and use of logarithms, elements of analytical geometry, and elements of statics. They must have some acquaintance with the practice of design.

The course of studies last three years, and instruction is gratuitous.

6. *School of master workmen in Mines* at Alais. This school is for educating foremen of mines, who shall have sufficient practical skill to guide the workmen, and enough theoretical knowledge to understand and execute the orders of the Director of the mine. The candidate for admission must be 16 years old, and must be able to cipher and understand the metrical system of weights and measures. The studies continue through two years, at the end of which the certificate of master miner is given to those who are qualified for it.

7. *School of Miners at Saint Etienne.* This institution is designed to train directors of mines, metallurgical establishments, &c. No one can be admitted who is less than 16 or more than 25 years of age. The preliminary examination requires a knowledge of the French language, arithmetic, elementary geometry and algebra, and the elements of linear design. The course of instruction, lasting three years is gratuitous. Certificates of capacity are awarded at its close.

8. *Imperial School of Forestry*, at Nancy. This institution is to train young men for the service of the administration of forests, a department of the government peculiarly important in France, on account of the high price of fuel, timber, &c. Pupils seeking admission, must be not less than 19 years of age, and not more than 22.

They must be free from all physical infirmities and disease, and must have received the degree of *Bachelier ès Sciences*, or a certificate of corresponding proficiency, and must also pass a satisfactory examination in geometry, trigonometry, physics, chemistry, cosmography mechanics, history and geography of France, and the German language. They must also write a French grammatical exercise, a Latin version, a German theme, and must evince a knowledge of linear and imitative design.

The course of studies lasts two years. At its termination, students who have passed a satisfactory examination have the rank of *garde général* of forests, and have a right to the vacancies occurring in the employments of that trade. They receive, provisionally, the salary of *garde général adjoint*, and are employed in the administration.

9. *The Imperial School of Bridges and Roads*, (Ponts et Chausées,) at Paris, is designed to train engineers of bridges and roads for the service of the government. Such pupils are received only from the Polytechnic school, but others, not intended for the public service, may also be admitted. The subjects of study are, construction of roads, rail-roads, canals, bridges, harbors, improvement of rivers, civil architecture, applied mechanics, agricultural hydraulics, etc.

Candidates for admission must be between 18 and 25 years of age, and must pass a triple examination, the highest studies in which are analytical and descriptive geometry, differential and integral calculus, mechanics, architecture, physics, and chemistry.

10. *Imperial Polytechnic School*, at Paris. In this institution young men are trained for the following services: military and naval artillery and engineering, the corps of hydographical engineers, the commissariat of the marine, the corps of the *Etat Major*, roads and bridges, mines, administration of tobacco, telegraphic lines, &c.; in short, those public services which demand a knowledge of physical, chemical, and mathematical sciences. Candidates for admission must be born in France or naturalized, must be between 16 and 20 years of age, and must have received the degree of *Bachelier ès Sciences*. They must pass a written and oral examination in various studies, including trigonometry, analytical and descriptive geometry, mechanics, physics, and chemistry, the French and German languages, &c. The studies continue through two years. The pupils are under military discipline.

11. *Conservatory of Arts and Trades, at Paris.* In connection with this great Industrial Museum, lectures are annually given by eminent professors, in the following departments: Geometry applied to the Arts, descriptive Geometry, Mechanics applied to the Arts, Physics

applied to the arts, chemistry applied to industry, chemistry applied to the arts, agricultural chemistry, zoölogy applied to agriculture and industry, agriculture, ceramic arts, spinning and weaving, dyeing, civil constructions, Industrial administration and statistics, industrial legislation.

Such are the principal higher schools for special scientific instruction. Subordinate schools, more directly practical in their character, have naturally arisen all over the land, some established by public, some by private enterprise. Among the former may be mentioned nearly fifty farm-schools, (fermes écoles,) and over forty schools of navigation, (hydrographie,) established in the principal maritime towns of the empire, for training captains and masters for commercial vessels.

No notice has been given in this article to the schools of design, of the fine arts, and of music, for which liberal provision is also made by the government.

SUBJECTS AND METHODS OF INSTRUCTION IN MATHEMATICS,

AS PRESCRIBED FOR ADMISSION TO THE POLYTECHNIC SCHOOL OF PARIS.

BY W. M. GILLESPIE, LL.D.,

Professor of Civil Engineering in Union College.

CONTENTS.

SUBJECTS AND METHODS OF INSTRUCTION

IN MATHEMATICS AS PRESCRIBED FOR ADMISSION TO THE POLYTECHNIC SCHOOL OF FRANCE.

"L'École Polytechnique" is too well known, by name at least, to need eulogy in this journal. Its course of instruction has long been famed for its completeness, precision, and adaptation to its intended objects. But this course had gradually lost somewhat of its symmetrical proportions by the introduction of some new subjects and the excessive development of others. The same defects had crept into the programme of the subjects of examination for admission to the school. Influenced by these considerations, the Legislative Assembly of France, by the law of June 5th, 1850, appointed a "*Commission*" to revise the programmes of admission and of internal instruction. The President of the Commission was Thenard, its "Reporter" was Le Verrier, and the other nine members were worthy to be their colleagues. They were charged to avoid the error of giving to young students, subjects and methods of instruction "too elevated, too abstract, and above their comprehension;" to see that the course prescribed should be "adapted, not merely to a few select spirits, but to average intelligences;" and to correct "the excessive development of the preparatory studies, which had gone far beyond the end desired."

The Commission, by M. Le Verrier, prepared an elaborate report of 440 quarto pages, only two hundred copies of which were printed, and these merely for the use of the authorities. A copy belonging to a deceased member of the Commission (the lamented Professor *Theodore Olivier*), having come into the hands of the present writer, he has thought that some valuable hints for our use in this country might be drawn from it, presenting as it does a precise and thorough course of mathematical instruction, adapted to any latitude, and arranged in the most perfect order by such competent authorities. He has accordingly here presented, in a condensed form, the opinions of the Commission on *the proper subjects for examination in mathematics, preparatory to admission to the Polytechnic School, and the best methods of teaching them.*

The subjects which will be discussed are Arithmetic; Geometry; Algebra; Trigonometry; Analytical Geometry; Descriptive Geometry.

I. ARITHMETIC.

A knowledge of Arithmetic is indispensable to every one. The merchant, the workman, the engineer, all need to know how to calculate with rapidity and precision. The useful character of arithmetic indicates that its methods should admit of great simplicity, and that its teaching should be most carefully freed from all needless complication. When we enter into the spirit of the methods of arithmetic, we perceive that they all flow clearly and simply from the very principles of numeration, from some precise definitions, and from certain ideas of relations between numbers, which all minds easily perceive, and which they even possessed in advance, before their teacher made them recognize them and taught them to class them in a methodical and fruitful order. We therefore believe that there is no one who is not capable of receiving, of understanding, and of enjoying well-arranged and well-digested arithmetical instruction.

But the great majority of those who have received a liberal education do not possess this useful knowledge. Their minds, they say, are not suited to the study of mathematics. They have found it impossible to bend themselves to the study of those abstract sciences whose barrenness and dryness form so striking a contrast to the attractions of history, and the beauties of style and of thought in the great poets; and so on.

Now, without admitting entirely the justice of this language, we do not hesitate to acknowledge, that the teaching of elementary mathematics has lost its former simplicity, and assumed a complicated and pretentious form, which possesses no advantages and is full of inconveniences. The reproach which is cast upon the sciences in themselves, we out-and-out repulse, and apply it only to the vicious manner in which they are now taught.

Arithmetic especially is only an instrument, a tool, the theory of which we certainly ought to know, but the practice of which it is above all important most thoroughly to possess. The methods of analysis and of mechanics, invariably lead to solutions whose applications require reduction into numbers by arithmetical calculations. We may add that the numerical determination of the final result is almost always indispensable to the clear and complete comprehension of a method ever so little complicated. Such an application, either by the more complete condensation of the ideas which it requires, or by its fixing the mind on the subject more precisely and clearly, develops a crowd of remarks which otherwise would not have been made, and it thus contributes to facilitate the comprehension of theories in such an efficacious manner that the time given to the numerical work is more than regained by its being no longer necessary to return incessantly to new explanations of the same method.

The teaching of arithmetic will therefore have for its essential object, to make the pupils acquire the habit of calculation, so that they may be able to make an easy and continual use of it in the course of their studies. The theory of the operations must be given to them with clearness and precision; not only that they may understand the mechanism of those operations, but because, in almost all questions, the application of the methods calls for great attention and continual discussion, if we would arrive at a result in which we can confide. But at the same time every useless theory must be carefully removed, so as not to distract the attention of the pupil, but to devote it entirely to the essential objects of this instruction.

It may be objected that these theories are excellent exercises to form the mind of the pupils. We answer that such an opinion may be doubted for more than one reason, and that, in any case, exercises on useful subjects not being wanting in the immense field embraced by mathematics, it is quite superfluous to create, for the mere pleasure of it, difficulties which will never have any useful application.

Another remark we think important. It is of no use to arrive at a numerical result, if we cannot answer for its correctness. The teaching of calculation should include, as an essential condition, that the pupils should be shown how every result, deduced from a series of arithmetical operations, may always be controlled in such a way that we may have all desirable certainty of its correctness; so that, though a pupil may and must often make mistakes, he may be able to discover them himself, to correct them himself, and never to present, at last, any other than an exact result.

The *Programme* given below is made very minute to avoid the evils which resulted from the brevity of the old one. In it, the limits of the matter required not being clearly defined, each teacher preferred to extend them excessively, rather than to expose his pupils to the risk of being unable to answer certain questions. The examiners were then naturally led to put the questions thus offered to them, so to say; and thus the preparatory studies grew into excessive and extravagant development. These abuses could be remedied only by the publication of programmes so detailed, that the limits within which the branches required for admission must be restricted should be so apparent to the eyes of all, as to render it impossible for the examiners to go out of them, and thus to permit teachers to confine their instruction within them.

The new programme for arithmetic commences with the words Decimal numeration. This is to indicate that the Duodecimal numeration will not be required.

The only practical verification of Addition and Multiplication, is to recommence these operations in a different order.

The Division of whole numbers is the first question considered at all difficult. This difficulty arises from the complication of the methods by which division is taught. In some books its explanation contains twice as many reasons as is necessary. The mind becomes confused by such instruction, and no longer understands what is a demonstration, when it sees it continued at the moment when it appeared to be finished. In most cases the demonstration is excessively complicated and does not follow the same order as the practical rule, to which it is then necessary to return. There lies the evil, and it is real and profound.

The phrase of the programme, Division of whole numbers, intends that the pupil shall be required to explain the practical rule, and be able to use it in a familiar and rapid manner. We do not present any particular mode of demonstration, but, to explain our views, we will indicate how we would treat the subject if we were making the detailed programme of a *course* of arithmetic, and not merely that of an *examination.* It would be somewhat thus:

"The quotient may be found by addition, subtraction, multiplication;

"Division of a number by a number of one figure, when the quotient is less than 10;

"Division of any number by a number less than 10;

"Division of any two numbers when the quotient has only one figure;

"Division in the most general case.

"*Note.*—The practical rule may be entirely explained by this consideration, that by multiplying the divisor by different numbers, we see if the quotient is greater or less than the multiplier."

The properties of the Divisors of numbers, and the decomposition of a number into prime factors should be known by the student. But here also we recommend simplicity. The theory of the greatest common divisor, for example, has no need to be given with all the details with which it is usually surrounded, for it is of no use in practice.

The calculation of Decimal numbers is especially that in which it is indispensable to exercise students. Such are the numbers on which they will generally have to operate. It is rare that the data of a question are whole numbers; usually they are decimal numbers which are not even known with rigor, but only with a given decimal approximation; and the result which is sought is to deduce from these, other decimal numbers, themselves exact to a certain degree of approximation, fixed by the conditions of the problem. It is thus that this subject should be taught. The pupil should not merely learn how, in one or two cases, he can obtain a result to within $\frac{1}{n}$, n being any number, but how to arrive by a practicable route to results which are exact to within a required decimal, and on the correctness of which they can depend.

Let us take decimal multiplication for an example. Generally the pupils do not know any other rule than "to multiply one factor by the other, without noticing the decimal point, except to cut off on the right of the product as many decimal figures as there are in the two factors." The rule thus enunciated is methodical, simple, and apparently easy. But, in reality, it is practically of a repulsive length, and is most generally inapplicable.

Let us suppose that we have to multiply together two numbers having each six decimals, and that we wish to know the product also to the sixth decimal. The above rule will give twelve decimals, the last six of which, being useless, will have caused by their calculation the loss of precious time. Still farther; when a factor of a product is given with six decimals, it is because we have stopped in its determination at that degree of approximation, neglecting the following decimals; whence it results that several of the decimals situated on the right of the calculated product are not those which would belong to the rigorous product. What then is the use of taking the trouble of determining them?

We will remark lastly that if the factors of the product are incommensurable, and if it is necessary to convert them into decimals before effecting the multiplication, we should not know how far we should carry the approximation of the factors before applying the above rule. It will therefore be necessary to teach the pupils the abridged methods by which we succeed, at the same time, in using fewer figures and in knowing the real approximation of the result at which we arrive.

Periodical decimal fractions are of no use. The two elementary questions of the programme are all that need be known about them.

The Extraction of the square root must be given very carefully, especially that of decimal numbers. It is quite impossible here to observe the rule of having in the square twice as many decimals as are required in the root. That rule is in fact impracticable when a series of operations is to be effected. "When a number N increases by a comparatively small quantity d, the square of that number increases very nearly as $2Nd$." It is thus that we determine the approximation with which a number must be calculated so that its square root may afterwards be obtained with the necessary exactitude. This supposes that before determining the square with all necessary precision, we have a suitable lower limit of the value of the root, which can always be done without difficulty.

The Cube root is included in the programme. The pupils should know this; but while it will be necessary to exercise them on the extraction of the square root by numerous examples, we should be very sparing of this in the cube root, and not go far beyond the mere theory. The calculations become too complicated and waste too much time. Logarithms are useful even for the square root; and quite indispensable for the cube root, and still more so for higher roots.

When a question contains only quantities which vary in the same ratio, or in an inverse ratio, it is immediately resolved by a very simple method, known under the name of *reduction to unity*. The result once obtained, it is indispensable to make the pupils remark that it is composed of the quantity which, among the data, is of the nature of that which is sought, multiplied successively by a series of abstract ratios between other quantities which also, taken two and two, are of the same nature. Hence flows the rule for writing directly the required result, without being obliged to take up again for each question the series of reasonings. This has the advantage, not only of saving time, but of better showing the spirit of the method, of making clearer the meaning of the solution, and of preparing for the subsequent use of formulas. The consideration of "homogeneity" conduces to these results.

We recommend teachers to abandon as much as possible the use of examples in abstract numbers, and of insignificant problems, in which the data, taken at random, have no connection with reality. Let the examples and the exercises presented to students always relate to objects which are found in the arts, in industry, in nature, in physics, in the system of the world. This will have many advantages. The precise meaning of the solutions will be better grasped. The pupils will thus acquire, without any trouble, a stock of precise and precious knowledge of the world which surrounds them. They will also more willingly engage in numerical calculations, when their attention is thus incessantly aroused and sustained, and when the result, instead of being merely a dry number, embodies information which is real, useful, and interesting.

The former arithmetical programme included the theory of *progressions* and *logarithms;* the latter being deduced from the former. But the theory of logarithms is again deduced in algebra from exponents, much the best method. This constitutes an objectionable "*double emploi.*" There is finally no good reason for retaining these theories in arithmetic.

The programme retains the questions which can be solved by making two arbitrary and successive hypotheses on the desired result. It is true that these questions can be directly resolved by means of a simple equation of the first degree; but we have considered that, since the resolution of problems by means of hypotheses, constitutes the most fruitful method really used in practice, it is well to accustom students to it the soonest possible. This is the more necessary, because teachers have generally pursued the opposite course, aiming especially to give their pupils direct solutions, without reflecting that the theory of these is usually much more complicated, and that the mind of the learner thus receives a direction exactly contrary to that which it will have to take in the end.

"Proportions" remain to be noticed.

In most arithmetics problems are resolved first by the method of "reduction to unity," and then by the theory of proportions. But beside the objection of the "*double emploi*," it is very certain that the method of reduction to unity presents, in their true light and in a complete and simple manner, all the questions of ratio which are the bases of arithmetical solutions; so that the subsequent introduction of proportions teaches nothing new to the pupils, and only presents the same thing in a more complicated manner. We therefore exclude from our programme of examination the solution of questions of arithmetic, presented under the special form which constitutes the theory of proportions.

This special form we would be very careful not to invent, if it had not already been employed. Why not say simply "The ratio of M to N is equal to that of P to Q," instead of hunting for this other form of enunciating the same idea, "M *is to* N *as* P *is to* Q"? It is in vain to allege the necessities of geometry; if we consider all the questions in which proportions are used, we shall see that the simple consideration of the equality of ratios is equally well adapted to the simplicity of the enunciation and the clearness of the demonstrations. However, since all the old books of geometry make use of proportions, we retain the properties of proportions at the end of our programme; but with this express reserve, that the examiners shall limit themselves to the simple properties which we indicate, and that they shall not demand any application of proportions to the solution of arithmetical problems.

PROGRAMME OF ARITHMETIC.

Decimal numeration.

Addition and subtraction of whole numbers.

Multiplication of whole numbers.—Table of Pythagoras.—The product of several whole numbers does not change its value, in whatever order the multiplications are effected.—To multiply a number by the product of several factors, it is sufficient to multiply successively by the factors of the product.

Division of whole numbers.—To divide a number by the product of several factors, it is sufficient to divide successively by the factors of the product.

Remainders from dividing a whole number by 2, 3, 5, 9, and 11.—Applications to the characters of divisibility by one of those numbers; to the verification of the product of several factors; and to the verification of the quotient of two numbers.

Prime numbers. Numbers prime to one another.

To find the greatest common divisor of two numbers.—If a number divides a product of two factors, and if it is prime to one of the factors, it divides the other.—To decompose a number into its prime factors.—To determine the smallest number divisible by given numbers.

Vulgar fractions.

A fraction does not alter in value when its two terms are multiplied or divided by the same number. Reduction of a fraction to its simplest expression. Reduction of several fractions to the same denominator. Reduction to the smallest common denominator.—To compare the relative values of several fractions.

Addition and subtraction of fractions.—Multiplication. Fractions of fractions.—Division.

Calculation of numbers composed of an entire part and a fraction.

Decimal numbers.

Addition and subtraction.

Multiplication and division.—How to obtain the product of the quotient to within a unit of any given decimal order.

To reduce a vulgar fraction to a decimal fraction.—When the denominator of an irreducible fraction contains other factors than 2 and 5, the fraction cannot be exactly reduced to decimals; and the quotient, which continues indefinitely, is periodical.

To find the vulgar fraction which generates a periodical decimal fraction: 1° when the decimal fraction is simply periodical; 2° when it contains a part not periodical.

System of the new measures.

Linear Measures.—Measures of surface.—Measures of volume and capacity.—Measures of weight.—Moneys.—Ratios of the principal foreign measures (England, Germany, United States of America) to the measures of France.

Of ratios. Resolution of problems.

General notions on quantities which vary in the same ratio or in an inverse ratio.—Solution, by the method called *Reduction to unity*, of the simplest questions in which such quantities are considered.—To show the homogeneity of the results which are arrived at; thence to deduce the general rule for writing directly the expression of the required solution.

Simple interest.—General formula, the consideration of which furnishes the solution of questions relating to simple interest.—Of discount, as practised in commerce.

To divide a sum into parts proportional to given numbers.

Of questions which can be solved by two arbitrary and successive hypotheses made on the desired result.

Of the square and of the square root. Of the cube and of the cube root.

Formation of the square and the cube of the sum of two numbers.—Rules for extracting the square root and the cube root of a whole number.—If this root is not entire, it cannot be exactly expressed by any number, and is called incommensurable.

Square and cube of a fraction.—Extraction of the square root and cube root of vulgar fractions.

Any number being given, either directly, or by a series of operations which permit only an approximation to its value by means of decimals, how to extract the square root or cube root of that number, to within any decimal unit.

Of the proportions called geometrical.

In every proportion the product of the extremes is equal to the product of the means.—Reciprocal proportion.—Knowing three terms of a proportion to find the fourth.—Geometrical mean of two numbers.—How the order of the terms of a proportion can be inverted without disturbing the proportion.

When two proportions have a common ratio, the two other ratios form a proportion.

In any proportion, each antecedent may be increased or diminished by its consequent without destroying the proportion.

When the corresponding terms of several proportions are multiplied together, the f ur products form a new proportion.—The same powers or the same roots of four numbers in proportion form a new proportion.

In a series of equal ratios, the sum of any number of antecedents and the sum of their consequents are still in the same ratio.

II. GEOMETRY

Some knowledge of Geometry is, next to arithmetic, most indispensable to every one, and yet very few possess even its first principles. This is the fault of the common system of instruction. We do not pay sufficient regard to the natural notions about straight lines, angles, parallels, circles, etc., which the young have acquired by looking around them, and which their minds have unconsciously considered before making them a regular study. We thus waste time in giving a dogmatic form to truths which the mind seizes directly.

The illustrious *Clairaut* complains of this, and of the instruction commencing always with a great number of definitions, postulates, axioms, and preliminary principles, dry and repulsive, and followed by propositions equally uninteresting. He also condemns the profusion of self-evident propositions, saying, "It is not surprising that Euclid should give himself the trouble to demonstrate that two circles which intersect have not the same centre; that a triangle situated within another has the sum of its sides smaller than that of the sides of the triangle which contains it; and so on. That geometer had to convince obstinate sophists, who gloried in denying the most evident truths. It was therefore necessary that geometry, like logic, should then have the aid of formal reasonings, to close the mouths of cavillers; but in our day things have changed face; all reasoning about what mere good sense decides in advance is now a pure waste of time, and is fitted only to obscure the truth and to disgust the reader."

Bezout also condemns the multiplication of the number of theorems, propositions, and corollaries; an array which makes the student dizzy, and amid which he is lost. All that follows from a principle should be given in natural language as far as possible, avoiding the dogmatic form. It is true that some consider the works of Bezout deficient in rigor, but he knew better than any one what really was a demonstration. Nor do we find in the works of the great old masters less generality of views, less precision, less clearness of conception than in modern treatises. Quite the contrary indeed.

We see this in Bezout's *definition of a right line*—that it tends continually towards one and the same point; and in that of *a curved line*—that it is the trace of a moving point, which turns aside infinitely little at each step of its progress; definitions most fruitful in consequences. When we define a right line as the shortest path from one point to another, we enunciate a property of that line which is of no use for demonstrations. When we define a curved line as one which is neither straight nor composed of straight lines, we enunciate two negations which can lead to no result, and which have no connection with the peculiar nature of the curved line. Bezout's definition, on the contrary, enters into the nature of the object to be defined, seizes its mode of being, its character, and puts the reader immediately in possession of the general idea from which are afterwards deduced the properties of curved lines and the construction of their tangents.

So too when Bezout says that, in order to form an exact idea of an angle, it is necessary to consider the movement of a line turning around one of its points, he gives an idea at once more just and more fruitful in consequences, both mathematical and mechanical, than that which is limited to saying, that the indefinite space comprised between two straight lines which meet in a point, and which may be regarded as prolonged indefinitely, is called an *angle;* a definition not very easily comprehended and absolutely useless for ulterior explanations, while that of Bezout is of continual service.

We therefore urge teachers to return, in their demonstrations, to the simplest ideas, which are also the most general; to consider a demonstration as finished and complete when it has evidently caused the truth to enter into the mind of the pupil, and to add nothing merely for the sake of silencing sophists.

Referring to our Programme of Geometry, given below, our first comments relate to the "Theory of parallels." This is a subject on which all students fear to be examined; and this being a general feeling, it is plain that it is not their fault, but that of the manner in which this subject is taught. The omission of the natural idea of the constant direction of the right line (as defined by Bezout) causes the complication of the first elements; makes it necessary for Legendre to demonstrate that all right angles are equal (a proposition whose meaning is rarely understood); and is the real source of all the pretended difficulties of the theory of parallels. These difficulties are now usually avoided by the admission of a *postulate*, after the example of Euclid, and to regulate the practice in that matter, we have thought proper to prescribe that this proposition—*Through a given point only a single parallel to a right line can be drawn*—should be admitted purely and simply, without demonstration, and as a direct consequence of our idea of the nature of the right line.

We should remark that the order of ideas in our programme supposes the properties of lines established without any use of the properties of surfaces. We think that, in this respect, it is better to follow Lacroix than Legendre.

When we prove thus that three parallels always divide two right lines into proportional parts, this proposition can be extended to the case in which the ratio of the parts is incommensurable, either by the method called *Reductio ad absurdum*, or by the method of *Limits*. We especially recommend the use of the latter method. The former has in fact nothing which satisfies the mind, and we should never have recourse to it, for it is always possible to do without it. When we have proved to the pupil that a desired quantity, X, cannot be either larger or smaller than A, the pupil is indeed forced to admit that X and A are equal; but that does not make him understand or feel why that equality exists. Now those demonstrations which are of such a nature that, once given, they disappear, as it were, so as to leave to the proposition demonstrated the character of a truth evident *à priori*, are those which should be carefully sought for, not only because they make that truth better felt, but because they better prepare the mind for conceptions of a more elevated order. The method of limits, is, for a certain number of questions, the only one which possesses this characteristic—that the demonstration is closely connected with the essential nature of the proposition to be established.

In reference to the relations which exist between the sides of a triangle and the segments formed by perpendiculars let fall from the summits, we will, once for all, recommend to the teacher, to exercise his students in making numerical applications of relations of that kind, as often as they shall present themselves in the course of geometry. This is the way to cause their meaning to be well understood, to fix them in the mind of students, and to give these the exercise in numerical calculation to which we positively require them to be habituated.

The theory of similar figures has a direct application in the art of surveying for plans (*Lever des plans*). We wish that this application should be given to the pupils in detail; that they should be taught to range out and measure a straight line on the ground; that a graphometer should be placed in their hands; and that they should use it and the chain to obtain on the ground, for themselves, all the data necessary for the construction of a map, which they will present to the examiners with the calculations in the margins.

It is true that a more complete study of this subject will have to be subsequently made by means of trigonometry, in which calculation will give more precision than these graphical operations. But some pupils may fail to extend their studies to trigonometry (the course given for the Polytechnic school having become the model for general instruction in France), and those who do will thus learn that trigonometry merely gives means of more precise calculation. This application will also be an encouragement to the study of a science whose utility the pupil will thus begin to comprehend.

It is common to say that an angle is measured by the arc of a circle, described from its summit or centre, and intercepted between its sides. It is true that teachers add, that since a quantity cannot be measured except by one of the same nature, and since the arc of a circle is of a different nature from an angle, the preceding enunciation is only an abridgment of the proposition by which we find the ratio of an angle to a right angle. Despite this precaution, the unqualified enunciation which precedes, causes uncertainty in the mind of the pupil, and produces in it a lamentable confusion. We will say as much of the following enunciations: "A dihedral angle is measured by the plane angle included between its sides;" "The surface of a spherical triangle is measured by the excess of the sum of its three angles above two right angles," etc.; enunciations which have no meaning in themselves, and from which every trace of homogeneity has disappeared. Now that everybody is requiring that the students of the Polytechnic school should better understand the meaning of the formulas which they are taught, which requires that their homogeneity should always be apparent, this should be attended to from the beginning of their studies, in geometry as well as in arithmetic. The examiners must therefore insist that the pupils shall never give them any enunciations in which homogeneity is not preserved.

The proportionality of the circumferences of circles to their radii must be inferred *directly* from the proportionality of the perimeters of regular polygons, of the same number of sides, to their apothems. In like manner, from the area of a regular polygon being measured by half of the product of its perimeter by the radius of the inscribed circle, it must be *directly* inferred that the area of a circle is measured by half of the product of its circumference by its radius. For a long time, these properties of the circle were differently demonstrated by proving, for example, with Legendre, that the measure of the circle could not be either smaller or greater than that which we have just given, whence it had to be inferred that it must be equal to it. The "Council of improvement" finally decided that this method should be abandoned, and that the method of limits should alone be admitted, in the examinations, for demonstrations of this kind. This was a true advance, but it was not sufficient. It did not, as it should, go on to consider the circle, purely and simply, as the limit of a series of regular polygons, the number of whose sides goes on increasing to infinity, and to regard the circle as possessing every property demonstrated for polygons. Instead of this, they inscribed and circumscribed to the circle two polygons of the same number of sides, and proved that, by the multiplication of the number of the sides of these polygons, the difference of their areas might become smaller than any given quantity, and thence, finally, deduced the measure of the area of the circle; that is to say, they took away from the method of limits all its advantage as to simplicity, by not applying it *frankly*.

We now ask that this shall cease; and that we shall no longer reproach for want of rigor, the Lagranges, the Laplaces, the Poissons, and Leibnitz, who has given us this principle: that "A curvilinear figure may be regarded as equivalent to a polygon of an infinite number of sides; whence it follows that whatsoever can be demonstrated of such a polygon, no regard being paid to the number of its sides, the same may be asserted of the curve." This is the principle for *the most simple* application of which to the measure of the circle and of the round bodies we appeal.

Whatever may be the formulas which may be given to the pupils for the determination of the ratio of the circumference to the diameter (the "Method of isoperimeters" is to be recommended for its simplicity), they must be required to perform the calculation, so as to obtain at least two or three exact decimals. These calculations, made with logarithms, must be methodically arranged and presented at the examination. It may be known whether the candidate is really the author of the papers, by calling for explanations on some of the steps, or making him calculate some points afresh.

The enunciations relating to the measurement of areas too often leave indistinctness in the minds of students, doubtless because of their form. We desire to make them better comprehended, by insisting on their application by means of a great number of examples.

As one application, we require the knowledge of the methods of surveying for content (*arpentage*), differing somewhat from the method of triangulation, used in the surveying for plans (*lever des plans*). To make this application more fruitful, the ground should be bounded on one side by an irregular curve. The pupils will not only thus learn how to overcome this practical difficulty, but they will find, in the calculation of the surface by means of trapezoids, the first application of the method of quadratures, with which it is important that they should very early become familiar. This application will constitute a new sheet of drawing and calculations to be presented at the examination.

Most of our remarks on plane geometry apply to geometry of three dimensions. Care should be taken always to leave homogeneity apparent, and to make numerous applications to the measurement of volumes.

The theory of similar polyhedrons often gives rise in the examinations of the students to serious difficulties on their part. These difficulties belong rather to the form than to the substance, and to the manner in which each individual mind seizes relations of position; relations always easier to feel than to express. The examiners should be content with arriving at the results enunciated in our programme, by the shortest and easiest road.

The simplicity desired cannot however be attained unless all have a common starting-point, in the definition of similar polyhedrons. The best course is assuredly to consider that theory in the point of view in which it is employed in the arts, especially in sculpture; i. e. to conceive the given system of points, M, N, P, ... to have lines passing from them through a point S, the *pole of similitude*, and prolonged beyond it to M′, N′, P′, ... so that SM′, SN′, SP′, ... are proportional to SM, SN, SP, ... Then the points M′, N′, P′, ... form a system *similar* to M, N, P, ...

The areas and volumes of the cylinder, of the cone, and of the sphere must be deduced from the areas and from the volumes of the prism, of the pyramid, and of the polygonal sector, with the same simplicity which we have required for the measure of the surface of the circle, and for the same reasons. It is, besides, the only means of easily extending to cones and cylinders with any bases whatever, right or oblique, those properties of cones and cylinders,—right and with circular bases,—which are applicable to them.

Numerical examples of the calculations, by logarithms, of these areas and volumes, including the area of a spherical triangle, will make another sheet to be presented to the examiners.

PROGRAMME OF GEOMETRY.

1. OF PLANE FIGURES.

Measure of the distance of two points.—Two finite right lines being given, to find their common measure, or at least their approximate ratio.

Of angles.—Right, acute, obtuse angles.—Angles vertically opposite are equal.

Of triangles.—Angles and sides.—The simplest cases of equality.—Elementary problems on the construction of angles and of triangles.

Of perpendiculars and of oblique lines.

Among all the lines that can be drawn from a given point to a given right line, the perpendicular is the shortest, and the oblique lines are longer in proportion to their divergence from the foot of the perpendicular.

Properties of the isosceles triangle.—Problems on tracing perpendiculars.—Division of a given straight line into equal parts.

Cases of equality of right-angled triangles.

Of parallel lines.

Properties of the angles formed by two parallels and a secant.—Reciprocally, when these properties exist for two right lines and a common secant, the two lines are parallel.*—Through a given point, to draw a right line parallel to a given right line, or cutting it at a given angle.—Equality of angles having their sides parallel and their openings placed in the same direction.

* It will be admitted, as a postulate, that only one parallel to a given right line can pass through a given point.

Sum of the angles of a triangle.

The parts of parallels intercepted between parallels are equal, and reciprocally.

Three parallels always divide any two right lines into proportional parts. The ratio of these parts may be incommensurable.—Application to the case in which a right line is drawn, in a triangle, parallel to one of its sides.

To find a fourth proportional to three given lines.

The right line, which bisects one of the angles of a triangle, divides the opposite side into two segments proportional to the adjacent sides.

Of similar triangles.

Conditions of similitude.—To construct on a given right line, a triangle similar to a given triangle.

Any number of right lines, passing through the same point and met by two parallels, are divided by these parallels into proportional parts, and divide them also into proportional parts.—To divide a given right line in the same manner as another is divided.—Division of a right line into equal parts.

If from the right angle of a right-angled triangle a perpendicular is let fall upon the hypothenuse, 1° this perpendicular will divide the triangle into two others which will be similar to it, and therefore to each other; 2° it will divide the hypothenuse into two segments, such that each side of the right angle will be a mean proportional between the adjacent segment and the entire hypothenuse; 3° the perpendicular will be a mean proportional between the two segments of the hypothenuse.

In a right-angled triangle, the square of the number which expresses the length of the hypothenuse is equal to the sum of the squares of the numbers which express the lengths of the other two sides.

The three sides of any triangle being expressed in numbers, if from the extremity of one of the sides a perpendicular is let fall on one of the other sides, the square of the first side will be equal to the sum of the squares of the other two, *minus* twice the product of the side on which the perpendicular is let fall by the distance of that perpendicular from the angle opposite to the first side, if the angle is *acute*, and *plus* twice the same product, if this angle is *obtuse*.

Of polygons.

Parallelograms.—Properties of their angles and of their diagonals.

Division of polygons into triangles.—Sum of their interior angles.—Equality and construction of polygons.

Similar polygons.—Their decomposition into similar triangles.—The right lines similarly situated in the two polygons are proportional to the homologous sides of the polygons.—To construct, on a given line, a polygon similar to a given polygon.—The perimeters of two similar polygons are to each other as the homologous sides of these polygons.

Of the right line and the circumference of the circle.

Simultaneous equality of arcs and chords in the same circle.—The greatest arc has the greatest chord, and reciprocally.—Two arcs being given in the same circle or in equal circles, to find the ratio of their lengths.

Every right line drawn perpendicular to a chord at its middle, passes through the centre of the circle and through the middle of the arc subtended by the chord.—Division of an arc into two equal parts.—To pass the circumference of a circle through three points not in the same right line.

The tangent at any point of a circumference is perpendicular to the radius passing through that point.

The arcs intercepted in the same circle between two parallel chords, or between a tangent and a parallel chord, are equal.

Measure of angles.

If from the summits of two angles two arcs of circles be described with the same radius, the ratio of the arcs included between the sides of each angle will be the same as that of these angles.—Division of the circumference into degrees, minutes, and seconds.—Use of the protractor.

An angle having its summit placed, 1° at the centre of a circle; 2° on the circumference of that circle; 3° within the circle between the centre and the circumference; 4° without the circle, but so that its sides cut the circumference; to determine the ratio of that angle to the right angle, by the consideration of the arc included between its sides.

From a given point without a circle, to draw a tangent to that circle.

To describe, on a given line, a segment of a circle capable of containing a given angle.

To make surveys for plans. (*Lever des plans.*)

Tracing a straight line on the ground.—Measuring that line with the chain.

Measuring angles with the graphometer.—Description of it.

Drawing the plan on paper.—Scale of reduction.—Use of the rule, the triangle, and the protractor.

To determine the distance of an inaccessible object, with or without the graphometer.

Three points, A, B, C, being situated on a smooth surface and represented on a map, to find thereon the point P from which the distances A B and A C have been seen under given angles. "The problem of the three points." "The *Trilinear* problem."

Of the contact and of the intersection of circles.

Two circles which pass through the same point of the right line which joins their centres have in common only that point in which they touch; and reciprocally, if two circles touch, their centres and the point of contact lie in the same right line.

Conditions which must exist in order that two circles may intersect.

Properties of the secants of the circle.

Two secants which start from the same point without the circle, being prolonged to the most distant part of the circumference, are reciprocally proportional to their exterior segments.—The tangent is a mean proportional between the secant and its exterior segment.

Two chords intersecting within a circle divide each other into parts reciprocally proportional.—The line perpendicular to a diameter and terminated by the circumference, is a mean proportional between the two segments of the diameter.

A chord, passing through the extremity of the diameter, is a mean proportional between the diameter and the segment formed by the perpendicular let fall from the other extremity of that chord.—To find a mean proportional between two given lines.

To divide a line in extreme and mean ratio.—The length of the line being given numerically, to calculate the numerical value of each of the segments.

Of polygons inscribed and circumscribed to the circle.

To inscribe or circumscribe a circle to a given triangle.

Every regular polygon can be inscribed and circumscribed to the circle.

A regular polygon being inscribed in a circle, 1° to inscribe in the same circle a polygon of twice as many sides, and to find the length of one of the sides of the second polygon; 2° to circumscribe about the circle a regular polygon of the same number of sides, and to express the side of the circumscribed polygon by means of the side of the corresponding inscribed polygon.

To inscribe in a circle polygons of 4, 8, 16, 32......sides.

To inscribe in a circle polygons of 3, 6, 12, 24, ...sides.

To inscribe in a circle polygons of 5, 10, 20, 40.....sides.

To inscribe in a circle polygons of 15, 30, 60.......sides.

Regular polygons of the same number of sides are similar, and their perimeters are to each other as the radii of the circles to which they are inscribed or circumscribed.—The circumferences of circles are to each other as their radii.

To find the approximate ratio of the circumference to the diameter.

Of the area of polygons and of that of the circle.

Two parallelograms of the same base and of the same height are equivalent.—Two triangles of the same base and height are equivalent.

The area of a rectangle and that of a parallelogram are equal to the product of the base by the height.—What must be understood by that enunciation.—The area of a triangle is measured by half of the product of the base by the height.

To transform any polygon into an equivalent square.—Measure of the area of a polygon.—Measure of the area of a trapezoid.

The square constructed on the hypothenuse of a right-angled triangle is equivalent to the sum of the squares constructed on the other two sides.—The squares constructed on the two sides of the right angle of a right-angled triangle and on the hypothenuse are to each other as the adjacent segments and entire hypothenuse.

The areas of similar polygons are to each other as the squares of the homologous sides of the polygons.

Notions on surveying for content (*arpentage*).—Method of decomposition into triangles.—Simpler method of decomposition into trapezoids.—Surveyor's cross.—Practical solution, when the ground is bounded, in one or more parts, by a curved line.

The area of a regular polygon is measured by half of the product of its perimeter by the radius of the inscribed circle.—The area of a circle is measured by half of the product of the circumference by the radius.—The areas of circles are to each other as the squares of the radii.

The area of a sector of a circle is measured by half of the product of the arc by the radius.—Measure of the area of a segment of a circle.

2. OF PLANES AND BODIES TERMINATED BY PLANE SURFACES.

Conditions required to render a right line and a plane respectively perpendicular.
Of all the lines which can be drawn from a given point to a given plane, the perpendicular is the shortest, and the oblique lines are longer in proportion to their divergence from the foot of the perpendicular.
Parallel right lines and planes.—Angles which have their sides parallel, and their openings turned in the same direction, are equal, although situated in different planes.
Dihedral angle.—How to measure the ratio of any dihedral angle to the right dihedral angle.
Planes perpendicular to each other.—The intersection of two planes perpendicular to a third plane, is perpendicular to this third plane.
Parallel planes.—When two parallel planes are cut by a third plane the intersections are parallel.—Two parallel planes have their perpendiculars common to both.
The shortest distance between two right lines, not intersecting and not parallel.
Two right lines comprised between two parallel planes are always divided into proportional parts by a third plane parallel to the first two.
Trihedral angle.—The sum of any two of the plane angles which compose a trihedral angle is always greater than the third.
The sum of the plane angles which form a convex polyhedral angle is always less than four right angles.
If two trihedral angles are formed by the same plane angles, the dihedral angles comprised between the equal plane angles are equal.—There may be absolute equality or simple symmetry between the two trihedral angles.

Of polyhedrons.
If two tetrahedrons have each a trihedral angle composed of equal and similarly arranged triangles, these tetrahedrons are equal. They are also equal if two faces of the one are equal to two faces of the other, are arranged in the same manner, and form with each other the same dihedral angle.
When the triangles which form two homologous trihedral angles of two tetrahedrons are similar, each to each, and similarly disposed, these tetrahedrons are similar. They are also similar if two faces of the one, making with each other the same angle as two faces of the other, are also similar to these latter, and are united by homologous sides and summits.
Similar pyramids.—A plane parallel to the base of a pyramid cuts off from it a pyramid similar to it.—To find the height of a pyramid when we know the dimension of its trunk with parallel bases.
Sections made in any two pyramids at the same distance from these summits are in a constant ratio.
Parallelopipedon.—Its diagonals.
Any polyhedron can always be divided into triangular pyramids.—Two bodies composed of the same number of equal and similarly disposed triangular pyramids, are equal.

Similar polyhedrons.
The homologous edges of similar polyhedrons are proportional; as are also the diagonals of the homologous faces and the interior diagonals of the polyhedrons.—The areas of similar polyhedrons are as the squares of the homologous edges.

Measure of volumes.
Two parallelopipedons of the same base and of the same height are equivalent in volume.
If a parallelogram be constructed on the base of a triangular prism, and on that parallelogram, taken as a base, there be constructed a parallelopipedon of the same height as the triangular prism, the volume of this prism will be half of the volume of the parallelopipedon.—Two triangular prisms of the same base and the same height are equivalent.
Two tetrahedrons of the same base and the same height are equivalent.
A tetrahedron is equivalent to the third of the triangular prism of the same base and the same height.
The volume of any parallelopipedon is equal to the product of its base by its height.—What must be understood by that enunciation.—The volume of any prism is equal to the product of its base by its height.
The volume of a tetrahedron and that of any pyramid are measured by the third of the product of the base by the height.
Volume of the truncated oblique triangular prism.
The volumes of two similar polyhedrons are to each other as the cubes of the homologous edges.

3. OF ROUND BODIES.

Of the right cone with circular base.

Sections parallel to the base.—Having the dimensions of the trunk of a cone with parallel bases, to find the height of the entire cone.

The area of a right cone is measured by half of the product of the circumference of its circular base by its side.—Area of a trunk of a right cone with parallel bases.

Volume of a pyramid inscribed in the cone.—The volume of a cone is measured by the third of the product of the area of its base by its height.*

Which of the preceding properties belong to the cone of any base whatever?

Of the right cylinder with circular base.

Sections parallel to the base.

The area of the convex surface of the right cylinder is measured by the product of the circumference of its base by its height.—This is also true of the right cylinder of any base.

Measure of the volume of a prism inscribed in the cylinder.—The volume of a right cylinder is measured by the product of the area of its base by its height.—This is also true of any cylinder, right or oblique, of any base whatever.

Of the sphere.

Every section of the sphere, made by a plane, is a circle.—Great circles and small circles.

In every spherical triangle any one side is less than the sum of the other two. The shortest path from one point to another, on the surface of the sphere, is the arc of a great circle which joins the two given points.

The sum of the sides of a spherical triangle, or of any spherical polygon, is less than the circumference of a great circle.

Poles of an arc of a great or small circle.—They serve to trace arcs of circles on the sphere.

Every plane perpendicular to the extremity of a radius is tangent to the sphere.

Measure of the angle of two arcs of great circles.

Properties of the polar or supplementary triangle.

Two spherical triangles situated on the same sphere, or on equal spheres, are equal in all their parts, 1° when they have an equal angle included between sides respectively equal; 2° when they have an equal side adjacent to two angles respectively equal; 3° when they are mutually equilateral; 4° when they are mutually equiangular. In these different cases the triangles may be equal, or merely symmetrical.

The sum of the angles of any spherical triangle is less than six, and greater than two, right angles.

The lune is to the surface of the sphere as the angle of that lune is to four right angles.

Two symmetrical spherical triangles are equivalent in surface.

The area of a spherical triangle is to that of the whole sphere as the excess of the sum of its angles above two right angles is to eight right angles.

When a portion of a regular polygon, inscribed in the generating circle of the sphere, turns around the diameter of that circle, the convex area engendered is measured by the product of its height by the circumference of the circle inscribed in the generating polygon.—The volume of the corresponding polygonal sector is measured by the area thus described, multiplied by the third of the radius of the inscribed circle.

The surface of a spherical zone is equal to the height of that zone multiplied by the circumference of a great circle.—The surface of the sphere is quadruple that of a great circle.

Every spherical sector is measured by the zone which forms its base, multiplied by the third of the radius. The whole sphere is measured by its surface multiplied by the third of its radius.†

---

* The volume of the cone is derived from that of the pyramid; and it is to be noted that the demonstration applies to the cone with closed base, whatever the figure of that base.

† Numerical examples on the areas and volumes of the round bodies, including the area of a spherical triangle, will be required by the examiners. The calculations will be made by logarithms.

III. ALGEBRA.

ALGEBRA is not, as are Arithmetic and Geometry, indispensable to every one. It should be very sparingly introduced into the general education of youth, and we would there willingly dispense with it entirely, excepting logarithms, if this would benefit the study of arithmetic and geometry. The programme of it which we are now to give, considers it purely in view of its utility to engineers, and we will carefully eliminate every thing not necessary for them.

Algebraical calculation presents no serious difficulty, when its students become well impressed with this idea, that every letter represents a number; and particularly when the consideration of negative quantities is not brought in at the outset and in an absolute manner. These quantities and their properties should not be introduced except as the solution of questions by means of equations causes their necessity to be felt, either for generalizing the rules of calculation, or for extending the meaning of the formulas to which it leads. CLAIRAUT pursues this course. He says, "I treat of the multiplication of negative quantities, that dangerous shoal for both scholars and teachers, only after having shown its necessity to the learner, by giving him a problem in which he has to consider negative quantities independently of any positive quantities from which they are subtracted. When I have arrived at that point in the problem where I have to multiply or divide negative quantities by one another, I take the course which was undoubtedly taken by the first analysts who have had those operations to perform and who have wished to follow a perfectly sure route: I seek for a solution of the problem which does not involve these operations; I thus arrive at the result by reasonings which admit of no doubt, and I thus see what those products or quotients of negative quantities, which had given me the first solution, must be." BEZOUT proceeds in the same way.

We recommend to teachers to follow these examples; not to speak to their pupils about negative quantities till the necessity of it is felt, and

* The true distinction between ALGEBRA and ARITHMETIC is so commonly overlooked that it may be well to present it here, in the words of Comte. "The complete solution of every question of calculation is necessarily composed of two successive parts, which have essentially distinct natures. In the first, the object is to *transform* the proposed equations, so as to make apparent the manner in which the unknown quantities are formed by the known ones; it is this which constitutes the *Algebraic* question. In the second, our object is *to find the value* of the formulas thus obtained; that is, to determine directly the values of the numbers sought, which are already represented by certain explicit functions of given numbers; this is the *Arithmetical* question. Thus the stopping-point of the algebraic part of the solution becomes the starting-point of the arithmetical part.

"ALGEBRA may therefore be defined as having for its object the *resolution of equations;* taking this expression in its full logical meaning, which signifies the transformation of *implicit* functions into equivalent *explicit* ones. In the same way ARITHMETIC may be defined as intended for *the determination of the values of functions*. Henceforth, therefore, we may call ALGEBRA *the Calculus of Functions*, and ARITHMETIC *the Calculus of Values*."

when they have become familiar with algebraic calculation; and above all not to lose precious time in obscure discussions and demonstrations, which the best theory will never teach students so well as numerous applications.

It has been customary to take up again, in algebra, the calculus of fractions, so as to generalize the explanations given in arithmetic, since the terms of literal fractions may be any quantities whatsoever. Rigorously, this may be well, but to save time we omit this, thinking it better to employ this time in advancing and exercising the mind on new truths, rather than in returning continually to rules already given, in order to imprint a new degree of rigor on their demonstration, or to give them an extension of which no one doubts.

The study of numerical equations of the first degree, with one or several unknown quantities, must be made with great care. We have required the solution of these equations to be made by the method of *substitution.* We have done this, not only because this method really comprehends the others, particularly that of *comparison,* but for this farther reason. In treatises on algebra, those equations alone are considered whose numerical coefficients and solutions are very simple numbers. It then makes very little difference what method is used, or in what order the unknown quantities are eliminated. But it is a very different thing in practice, where the coefficients are complicated numbers, given with decimal parts, and where the numerical values of these coefficients may be very different in the same equation, some being very great and some very small. In such cases the method of *substitution* can alone be employed to advantage, and that with the precaution of taking the value of the unknown quantity to be eliminated from that equation in which it has relatively the greatest coefficient. Now the method of *comparison* is only the method of substitution put in a form in which these precautions cannot be observed, so that in practice it will give bad results with much labor.

The candidates must present to the examiners the complete calculations of the resolution of four equations with four unknown quantities, made with all the precision permitted by the logarithmic tables of Callet, and the proof that that precision has been obtained. The coefficients must contain decimals and be very different from one another, and the elimination must be effected with the above precautions.

The teaching of the present day disregards too much the applicability of the methods given, provided only that they be elegant in their form; so that they have to be abandoned and changed when the pupils enter on practice. This disdain of practical utility was not felt by our great mathematicians, who incessantly turned their attention towards applications. Thus the illustrious Lagrange made suggestions like those just given; and Laplace recommended the drawing of curves for solving directly all kinds of numerical equations.

As to literal equations of the first degree, we call for formulas sufficient for the resolution of equations of two or three unknown quantities. Bezout's method of elimination must be given as a first application of that fruitful method of indeterminates. The general discussion of formulas will be confined to the case of two unknown quantities. The discussion of three equations with three unknown quantities, x, y, and z, in which the terms independent of the unknown quantities are null, will be made directly, by this simple consideration that the system then really includes only two unknown quantities, to wit, the ratios of x and y, for example, to z.

The resolution of inequalities of the first degree with one or more unknown quantities, was added to equations of the first degree some years ago. We do not retain that addition.

The equations of the second degree, like the first, must be very carefully given. In dwelling on the case where the coefficient of x^2 converges towards zero, it will be remarked that, when the coefficient is very small, the ordinary formula would give one of the roots by the difference of two numbers almost equal; so that sufficient exactness could not be obtained without much labor. It must be shown how that inconvenience may be avoided.

It is common to meet with expressions of which the maximum or the minimum can be determined by the consideration of an equation of the second degree. We retain the study of them, especially for the benefit of those who will not have the opportunity of advancing to the general theory of maxima and minima.

The theory of the algebraic calculation of imaginary quantities, given *à priori*, may, on the contrary, be set aside without inconvenience. It is enough that the pupils know that the different powers of $\sqrt{-1}$ continually reproduce in turn one of these four values, ± 1, $\pm\sqrt{-1}$. We will say as much of the calculation of the algebraic values of radicals, which is of no use. The calculation of their *arithmetical* values will alone be demanded. In this connection will be taught the notation of fractional exponents and that of negative exponents.

The theory of numbers has taken by degrees a disproportionate development in the examinations for admission; it is of no use in practice, and, besides, constitutes in the pure mathematics a science apart.

The theory of continued fractions at first seems more useful. It is employed in the resolution of algebraic equations, and in that of the exponential equation $a^x=b$. But these methods are entirely unsuited to practice, and we therefore omit this theory.

The theory of series, on the contrary, claims some farther developments. Series are continually met with in practice; they give the best solutions of many questions, and it is indispensable to know in what circumstances they can be safely employed.

We have so often insisted on the necessity of teaching students to calculate, as to justify the extent of the part of the programme relating to logarithms. We have suppressed the inapplicable method of determining logarithms by continued fractions, and have substituted the employment of the series which gives the logarithm of $n+1$, knowing that of n. To exercise the students in the calculation of the series, they should be made to determine the logarithms of the numbers from 1 to 10, from 101 to 110, and from 10,000 to 10,010, the object of these last being to show them with what rapidity the calculation proceeds when the numbers are large; the first term of the series is then sufficient, the variations of the logarithms being sensibly proportional to the variations of the numbers, within the limits of the necessary exactness. In the logarithmic calculations, the pupils will be exercised in judging of the exactness which they may have been able to obtain: the consideration of the numerical values of the proportional parts given in the tables is quite sufficient for this purpose, and is beside the only one which can be employed in practice.

The use of the sliding rule, which is merely an application of logarithms, gives a rapid and portable means of executing approximately a great number of calculations which do not require great exactness. We desire that the use of this little instrument should be made familiar to the candidates. This is asked for by all the professors of the "School of application," particularly those of Topography, of Artillery, of Construction, and of Applied Mechanics, who have been convinced by experience of the utility of this instrument, which has the greatest possible analogy with tables of logarithms.

Before entering on the subjects of higher algebra, it should be remembered that the reductions of the course which we have found to be so urgent, will be made chiefly on it. The general theory of equations has taken in the examinations an abnormal and improper development, not worth the time which it costs the students. We may add, that it is very rare to meet a numerical equation of a high degree requiring to be resolved, and that those who have to do this, take care not to seek its roots by the methods which they have been taught. These methods moreover are not applicable to transcendental equations, which are much more frequently found in practice.

The theory of the greatest common algebraic divisor, in its entire generality, is of no use, even in pure science, unless in the elimination between equations of any degree whatever. But this last subject being omitted, the greatest common divisor is likewise dispensed with.

It is usual in the general theory of algebraic equations to consider the derived polynomials of entire functions of x. These polynomials are in fact useful in several circumstances, and particularly in the theory of equal roots; and in analytical geometry, they serve for the discussion of curves and the determination of their tangents. But since transcendental curves are very often encountered in practice, we give in our programme the calculation of the derivatives of algebraic and fractional functions, and transcendental functions, logarithmic, exponential, and circular. This has been long called for, not only because it must be of great assistance in the teaching of analytical geometry, but also because it will facilitate the elementary study of the infinitesimal calculus.

We have not retrenched any of the general ideas on the composition of an entire polynomial by means of factors corresponding to its roots. We retain several theorems rather because they contain the germs of useful ideas than because of their practical utility, and therefore wish the examiners to restrict themselves scrupulously to the programme.

The essential point in practice is to be able to determine conveniently an incommensurable root of an algebraic or transcendental equation, when encountered. Let us consider first an algebraic equation.

All the methods which have for their object to separate the roots, or to approximate to them, begin with the substitution of the series of consecutive whole numbers, in the first member of the equation. The direct substitution becomes exceedingly complicated, when the numbers substituted become large. It may be much shortened, however, by deducing the results from one another by means of their differences, and guarding against any possibility of error, by verifying some of those results, those corresponding to the numbers easiest to substitute, such as ± 10, ± 20. The teacher should not fail to explain this to his pupils.

Still farther: let us suppose that we have to resolve an equation of the third degree, and that we have recognized by the preceding calculations the necessity of substituting, between the numbers 2 and 3, numbers differing by a tenth, either for the purpose of continuing to effect the separation of the roots, or to approximate nearer to a root comprised between 2 and 3. If we knew, for the result corresponding to the substitution of 2, the first, second, and third differences of the results of the new substitutions, we could thence deduce those results themselves with as much simplicity, as in the case of the whole numbers. The new third difference, for example, will be simply the thousandth part of the old third difference. We may also remark that there is no possibility of error, since, the numbers being deduced from one another, when we in this way arrive at the result of the substitution of 3, which has already been calculated, the whole work will thus be verified.

Let us suppose again that we have thus recognized that the equation has a root comprised between 2.3 and 2.4; we will approximate still nearer by substituting intermediate numbers, differing by 0.01, and employing the course just prescribed. As soon as the third differences can be neglected, the calculation will be finished at once, by the consideration of an equation of the second degree; or, if it is preferred to continue the approximations till the second differences in their turn may be neglected, the calculation will then be finished by a simple proportion.

When, in a transcendental equation $f(X)=0$, we have substituted in $f(X)$ equidistant numbers, sufficiently near to each other to allow the differences of the results to be neglected, commencing with a certain order, the 4th, for example, we may, within certain limits of x, replace the transcendental function by an algebraic and entire function of x, and thus reduce the search for the roots of $f(X)=0$ to the preceding theory.

Whether the proposed equation be algebraic or transcendental, we can thus, when we have obtained one root of it with a suitable degree of exactness, continue the approximation by the method of Newton.

PROGRAMME OF ALGEBRA.

Algebraic calculation.

Addition and subtraction of polynomials.—Reduction of similar terms.

Multiplication of monomials.—Use of exponents.—Multiplication of polynomials. Rule of the signs.—To arrange a polynomial.—Homogeneous polynomials.

Division of monomials. Exponent *zero.*—Division of polynomials. How to know if the operation will not terminate.—Division of polynomials when the dividend contains a letter which is not found in the divisor.

Equations of the first degree.

Resolution of numerical equations of the first degree with one or several unknown quantities by the method of substitution.—Verification of the values of the unknown quantities and of the degree of their exactness.

Of cases of impossibility or of indetermination.

Interpretation of negative values.—Use and calculation of negative quantities.

Investigation of general formulas for obtaining the values of the unknown quantities in a system of equations of the first degree with two or three unknown quantities.—Method of Bezout.—Complete discussion of these formulas for the case of two unknown quantities.—Symbols $\frac{m}{0}$ and $\frac{0}{0}$.

Discussion of three equations with three unknown quantities, in which the terms independent of the unknown quantities are null.

Equations of the second degree with one unknown quantity.

Calculus of radicals of the second degree.

Resolution of an equation of the second degree with one unknown quantity.—Double solution.—Imaginary values.

When, in the equation $ax^2+bx+c=0$, a converges towards 0, one of the roots increases indefinitely.—Numerical calculation of the two roots, when a is very small.

Decomposition of the trinomial x^2+px+q into factors of the first degree.—Relations between the coefficients and the roots of the equation $x^2+px+q=0$.

Trinomial equations reducible to the second degree.
Of the maxima and minima which can be determined by equations of the second degree.
Calculation of the *arithmetical* values of radicals.
Fractional exponents.—Negative exponents.

Of series.
Geometrical progressions.—Summation of the terms.
What we call a series.—Convergence and divergence.
A geometrical progression is convergent, when the ratio is smaller than unity; diverging, when it is greater.
The terms of a series may decrease indefinitely and the series not be converging.
A series, all the terms of which are positive, is converging, when the ratio of one term to the preceding one tends towards a *limit* smaller than unity, in proportion as the index of the rank of that term increases indefinitely.—The series is diverging when this *limit* is greater than unity. There is uncertainty when it is equal to unity.
In general, when the terms of a series decrease indefinitely, and are alternately positive and negative, the series is converging.

Combinations, arrangements, and permutations of m letters, when each combination must not contain the same letter twice.
Development of the entire and positive powers of a binomial.—General terms.
Development of $(a+b\sqrt{-1})^m$.
Limit towards which $\left(1+\frac{1}{m}\right)^m$ tends, when m increases indefinitely.
Summation of piles of balls.

Of logarithms and of their uses.
All numbers can be produced by forming all the powers of any positive number, greater or less than *one.*
General properties of logarithms.
When numbers are in geometrical progression, their logarithms are in arithmetical progression.
How to pass from one system of logarithms to another system.
Calculation of logarithms by means of the series which gives the logarithm of $n+1$, knowing that of n.—Calculation of Napierian logarithms.—To deduce from them those of Briggs. Modulus.
Use of logarithms whose base is 10.—Characteristics.—Negative characteristics. Logarithms entirely negative are not used in calculation.
A number being given, how to find its logarithm in the tables of Callet. A logarithm being given, how to find the number to which it belongs.—Use of the proportional parts.—Their application to appreciate the exactness for which we can answer.
Employment of the sliding rule.
Resolution of exponential equations by means of logarithms.
Compound interest. Annuities.

Derived functions.
Development of an entire function F $(x+h)$ of the binomial $(x+h)$.—Derivative of an entire function.—To return from the derivative to the function.
The derivative of a function of x is the limit towards which tends the ratio of the increment of the function to the increment h of the variable, in proportion as h tends towards zero.
Derivatives of trigonometric functions.
Derivatives of exponentials and of logarithms.
Rules to find the derivative of a sum, of a product, of a power, of a quotient of functions of x, the derivatives of which are known.

Of the numerical resolution of equations.
Changes experienced by an entire function $f(x)$ when x varies in a continuous manner.—When two numbers a and b substituted in an entire function $f(x)$ give results with contrary signs, the equation $f(x)=0$ has at least one real root not comprised between a and b. This property subsists for every species of function which remains continuous for all the values of x comprised between a and b.
An algebraic equation of uneven degree has at least one real root.—An algebraic equation of even degree, whose last term is negative, has at least two real roots.
Every equation $f(x)=0$, with coefficients either real or imaginary of the form $a+b\sqrt{-1}$, admits of a real or imaginary root of the same form. [Only the enunciation, and not the demonstration of this theorem, is required.]

If a is a root of an algebraic equation, the first member is divisible by $x-a$. An algebraic equation of the mth degree has always m roots real or imaginary, and it cannot admit more.—Decomposition of the first members into factors of the first degree. Relations between the coefficients of an algebraic equation and its roots.

When an algebraic equation whose coefficients are real, admits an imaginary root of the form $a+b\sqrt{-1}$, it has also for a root the conjugate expression $a-b\sqrt{-1}$.

In an algebraic expression, complete or incomplete, the number of the positive roots cannot surpass the number of the variations; consequence, for negative roots.

Investigation of the product of the factors of the first degree common to two entire functions of x.—Determination of the roots common to two equations, the first members of which are entire functions of the unknown quantity.

By what character to recognize that an algebraic equation has equal roots.—How we then bring its resolution to that of several others of lower degree and of unequal roots.

Investigation of the commensurable roots of an algebraic equation with entire coefficients.

When a series of equidistant numbers is substituted in an entire function of the mth degree, and differences of different orders between the results are formed, the differences of the mth order are constant.

Application to the separation of the roots of an equation of the third degree.—Having the results of the substitution of -1, 0, and $+1$, to deduce therefrom, by means of differences, those of all other whole numbers, positive or negative.—The progress of the calculation leads of itself to the limits of the roots.—Graphical representation of this method.

Substitution of numbers equidistant *by a tenth*, between two consecutive whole numbers, when the inspection of the first results has shown its necessity.—This substitution is effected directly, or by means of new differences deduced from the preceding.

How to determine, in continuing the approximation towards a root, at what moment the consideration of the first difference is sufficient to give that root with all desirable exactness, by a simple proportion.

The preceding method becomes applicable to the investigation of the roots of a transcendental equation $X=0$, when there have been substituted in the first member, numbers equidistant and sufficiently near to allow the differences of the results to be considered as constant, starting from a certain order.—Formulas of interpolation.

Having obtained a root of an algebraic or transcendental equation, with a certain degree of approximation, to approximate still farther by the method of Newton.

Resolution of two numerical equations of the second degree with two unknown quantities.

Decomposition of rational fractions into simple fractions.

IV. TRIGONOMETRY.

In explaining the use of trigonometrical tables, the pupil must be able to tell with what degree of exactness an angle can be determined by the logarithms of any of its trigonometrical lines. The consideration of the proportional parts will be sufficient for this. It will thus be seen that if the *sine* determines perfectly a small angle, the degree of exactness, which may be expected from the use of that line, diminishes as the angle increases, and becomes quite insufficient in the neighborhood of 90 degrees. It is the reverse for the *cosine*, which may serve very well to represent an angle near 90 degrees, while it would be very inexact for small angles. We see, then, that in our applications, we should distrust those formulas which give an angle by its sine or cosine. The *tangent* being alone exempt from these difficulties, we should seek, as far as possible, to resolve all questions by means of it. Thus, let us suppose that we know the hypothenuse and one of the sides of a right-angled triangle, the direct determination of the included angle will be given by a cosine, which will be wanting in exactness if the hypothenuse of the triangle does not differ much from the given side. In that case we should begin by calculating the third side, and then use it with the first side to determine the desired angle by means of its tangent. When two sides of a triangle and the included angle are given, the tangent of the half difference of the desired angles may be calculated with advantage; but we may also separately determine the tangent of each of them. When the three sides of a triangle are given, the best formula for calculating an angle, and the only one never at fault, is that which gives the tangent of half of it.

The surveying for plans, taught in the course of Geometry, employing only graphical methods of calculation, did not need any more accurate instruments than the chain and the graphometer; but now that trigonometry furnishes more accurate methods of calculation, the measurements on the ground require more precision. Hence the requirement for the pupil to measure carefully a base, to use telescopes, verniers, etc., and to make the necessary calculations, the ground being still considered as plane. But as these slow and laborious methods can be employed for only the principal points of the survey, the more expeditious means of the plane-table and compass will be used for the details.

In spherical trigonometry, all that will be needed in geodesy should be learned before admission to the school, so that the subject will not need to be again taken up. We have specially inscribed in the programme the relations between the angles and sides of a right-angled triangle, which must be known by the students; they are those which occur in practice. In tracing the course to be pursued in the resolution of the three cases of any triangles, we have indicated that which is in fact employed in the applications, and which is the most convenient. As to the rest, ambiguous cases never occur in practice, and therefore we should take care not to speak of them to learners.

In surveying, spherical trigonometry will now allow us to consider cases in which the signals are not all in the same plane, and to operate on uneven ground, obtain its projection on the plane of the horizon, and at the same time determine differences of level.

It may be remarked that Descriptive Geometry might supply the place of spherical trigonometry by a graphical construction, but the degree of exactitude of the differences of level thus obtained would be insufficient.

PROGRAMME OF TRIGONOMETRY.

1. PLANE TRIGONOMETRY.

Trigonometrical lines.—Their ratios to the radius are alone considered.—Relations of the trigonometric lines of the same angle.—Expressions of the sine and of the cosine in functions of the tangent.

Knowing the sines and the cosines of two arcs a and b, to find the sine and the cosine of their sum and of their difference.—To find the tangent of the sum or of the difference of two arcs, knowing the tangents of those arcs.

Expressions for sin. $2a$ and sin. $3a$; cos. $2a$ and cos. $3a$; tang. $2a$ and tang. $3a$.

Knowing sin. a or cos. a, to calculate sin. $\frac{1}{2}a$ and cos. $\frac{1}{2}a$.

Knowing tang. a, to calculate tang. $\frac{1}{2}a$.

Knowing sin. a, to calculate sin. $\frac{1}{3}a$.—Knowing cos. a, to calculate cos. $\frac{1}{3}a$.

Use of the formula $\cos. p + \cos. q = 2 \cos. \frac{1}{2}(p+q) \cos. \frac{1}{2}(p-q)$, to render logarithms applicable to the sum of two trigonometrical lines, sines or cosines.—To render logarithms applicable to the sum of two tangents.

Construction of the trigonometric tables.

Use in detail of the tables of Callet.—Appreciation, by the proportional parts, of the degree of exactness in the calculation of the angles.—Superiority of the tangent formulas.

Resolution of triangles.

Relations between the angles and the sides of a right-angled triangle, or of any triangle whatever.—When the three angles of a triangle are given, these relations determine only the ratios of the sides.

Resolution of right-angled triangles.—Of the case in which the hypothenuse and a side nearly equal to it are given.

Knowing a side and two angles of any triangle, to find the other parts, and also the surface of the triangle.

Knowing two sides a and b of a triangle and the included angle C, to find the other parts and also the surface of the triangle.—The tang. $\frac{1}{2}$(A—B) may be determined; or tang. A and tang. B directly.

Knowing the three sides a, b, c, to find the angles and the surface of the triangle.—Employment of the formula which gives tang. $\frac{1}{2}$A.

Application to surveying for plans.

Measurement of bases with rods.

Measurement of angles.—Description and use of the circle.—Use of the telescope to render the line of sight more precise.—Division of the circle.—Verniers.

Measurement and calculation of a system of triangles.—Reduction of angles to the centres of stations.

How to connect the secondary points to the principal system.—Use of the plane table and of the compass.

2. SPHERICAL TRIGONOMETRY.

Fundamental relations ($\cos. a = \cos. b \cos. c + \sin. b \sin. c \cos. A$) between the sides and the angles of a spherical triangle.

To deduce thence the relations $\sin. A : \sin. B = \sin. a : \sin. b$; $\cot. a \sin. b - \cot. A \sin. C = \cos. b \cos. C$, and by the consideration of the supplementary triangle $\cos. A = -\cos. B \cos. C + \sin. B \sin. C \cos. a$.

Right-angled triangles.—Formulas $\cos. a = \cos. b \cos. c$; $\sin. b = \sin. a \sin. B$; $\text{tang.}\, c = \text{tang.}\, a \cos. B$, and $\text{tang.}\, b = \sin. c\, \text{tang.}\, B$.

In a right-angled triangle the three sides are less than 90°, or else two of the sides are greater than 90°, and the third is less. An angle and the side opposite to it are both less than 90°, or both greater.

Resolution of any triangles whatever:

1° Having given their three sides a, b, c, or their three angles A, B, C.—Formulas tang. $\frac{1}{2}a$, and tang. $\frac{1}{2}$A, calculable by logarithms:

2° Having given two sides and the included angle, or two angles and the included side.—Formulas of Delambre:

3° Having given two sides and an angle opposite to one of them, or two angles and a side opposite to one of them. Employment of an auxiliary angle to render the formulas calculable by logarithms.

Applications.—Survey of a mountainous country.—Reduction of the base and of the angles to the horizon.—Determination of differences of level.

Knowing the latitude and the longitude of two points on the surface of the earth, to find the distance of those points.

V. ANALYTICAL GEOMETRY.

The important property of homogeneity must be given with clearness and simplicity.

The transformation of co-ordinates must receive some numerical applications, which are indispensable to make the student clearly see the meaning of the formulas.

The determination of tangents will be effected in the most general manner by means of the derivatives of the various functions, which we inserted in the programme of algebra. After having shown that this determination depends on the calculation of the derivative of the ordinate with respect to the abscissa, this will be used to simplify the investigation of the tangent to curves of the second degree and to curves whose equations contain transcendental functions. The discussion of these, formerly pursued by laborious indirect methods, will now become easy; and as curves with transcendental equations are frequently encountered, it will be well to exercise students in their discussion.

The properties of foci and of the directrices of curves of the second degree will be established directly, for each of the three curves, by means of the simplest equations of these curves, and without any consideration of the analytical properties of foci, with respect to the general equation of the second degree. With even greater reason will we dispense with examining whether curves of higher degree have foci, a question whose meaning even is not well defined.

We retained in algebra the elimination between two equations of the second degree with two unknown quantities, a problem which corresponds to the purely analytical investigation of the co-ordinates of the points of intersection of two curves of the second degree. The final equation is in general of the fourth degree, but we may sometimes dispense with calculating that equation. A graphical construction of the curves, carefully made, will in fact be sufficient to make known, approximately, the co-ordinates of each of the points of intersection; and when we shall have thus obtained an approximate solution, we will often be able to give it all the numerical rigor desirable, by successive approximations, deduced from the equations. These considerations will be extended to the investigation of the real roots of equations of any form whatever with one unknown quantity.

Analytical geometry of three dimensions was formerly entirely taught within the Polytechnic school, none of it being reserved for the course of admission. For some years past, however, candidates were required to know the equations of the right line in space, the equation of the plane, the solution of the problems which relate to it and the transformation of co-ordinates. But the consideration of surfaces of the second order was reserved for the interior teaching. We think it well to place this also among the studies to be mastered before admission, in accordance with the general principle now sought to be realized, of classing with them that double instruction which does not exact a previous knowledge of the differential calculus.

We have not, however, inserted here all the properties of surfaces of the second order, but have retained only those which it is indispensable to know and to retain. The transformation of rectilinear co-ordinates, for example, must be executed with simplicity, and the teacher must restrict himself to giving his pupils a succinct explanation of the course to be pursued; this will suffice to them for the very rare cases in which they may happen to have need of them. No questions will be asked relating to the general considerations, which require very complicated theoretical discussions, and especially that of the general reduction of the equation of the second degree with three variables. We have omitted from the problems relating to the right line and to the plane, the determination of the shortest distance of two right lines.

The properties of surfaces of the second order will be deduced from the equations of those surfaces, taken directly in the simplest forms. Among these properties, we place in the first rank, for their valuable applications, those of the surfaces which can be generated by the movement of a right line.

PROGRAMME OF ANALYTICAL GEOMETRY.

1. GEOMETRY OF TWO DIMENSIONS.

Rectilinear co-ordinates.—Position of a point on a plane.

Representation of geometric loci by equations.

Homogeneity of equations and of formulas.—Construction of algebraic expressions.

Transformation of rectilinear co-ordinates.

Construction of equations of the first degree.—Problems on the right line.

Construction of equations of the second degree.—Division of the curves which they represent into three classes.—Reduction of the equation to its simplest form by the change of co-ordinates.*

Problem of tangents.—The coefficient of inclination of the tangent to the curve, to the axis of the abscissas, is equal to the derivative of the ordinate with respect to the abscissa.

Of the ellipse.

Centre and axes.—The squares of the ordinates perpendicular to one of the axes are to each other as the products of the corresponding segments formed on that axis.

The ordinates perpendicular to the major axis are to the corresponding ordinates of the circle described on that axis as a diameter, in the constant ratio of the minor axis to the major.—Construction of the curve by points, by means of this property.

Foci; eccentricity of the ellipse.—The sum of the radii vectors drawn to any point of the ellipse is constant and equal to the major axis.—Description of the ellipse by means of this property.

* The students will apply these reductions to a numerical equation of the second degree, and will determine the situation of the new axes with respect to the original axes, by means of trigonometrical tables. They will show to the examiner the complete calculations of this reduction and the trace of the two systems of axes and of the curves.

Directrices.—The distance from each point of the ellipse to one of the foci, and to the directrix adjacent to that focus, are to each other as the eccentricity is to the major axis.

Equations of the tangent and of the normal at any point of the ellipse.*—The point in which the tangent meets one of the axes prolonged is independent of the length of the other axis.—Construction of the tangent at any point of the ellipse by means of this property.

The radii vectores, drawn from the foci to any point of the ellipse, make equal angles with the tangent at that point or the same side of it.—The normal bisects the angle made by the radii vectores with each other.—This property may serve to draw a tangent to the ellipse through a point on the curve, or through a point exterior to it.

The diameters of the ellipse are right lines passing through the centre of the curve.—The chords which a diameter bisects are parallel to the tangent drawn through the extremity of that diameter.—Supplementary chords. By means of them a tangent to the ellipse can be drawn through a given point on that curve or parallel to a given right line.

Conjugate diameters.—Two conjugate diameters are always parallel to supplementary chords, and reciprocally.—Limit of the angle of two conjugate diameters.—An ellipse always contains two equal conjugate diameters.—The sum of the squares of two conjugate diameters is constant.—The area of the parallelogram constructed on two conjugate diameters is constant.—To construct an ellipse, knowing two conjugate diameters and the angle which they make with each other.

Expression of the area of an ellipse in function of its axes.

Of the hyperbola.

Centre and axes.—Ratio of the squares of the ordinates perpendicular to the transverse axes.

Of foci and of directrices; of the tangent and of the normal; of diameters and of supplementary chords.—Properties of these points and of these lines, analogous to those which they possess in the ellipse.

Asymptotes of the hyperbola.—The asymptotes coincide with the diagonals of the parallelogram formed on any two conjugate diameters.—The portions of a secant comprised between the hyperbola and its asymptotes are equal.—Application to the tangent and to its construction.

The rectangle of the parts of a secant, comprised between a point of the curve and the asymptotes, is equal to the square of half of the diameter to which the secant is parallel.

Form of the equation of the hyperbola referred to its asymptotes.

Of the parabola.

Axis of the parabola.—Ratio of the squares of the ordinates perpendicular to the axis.

Focus and directrix of the parabola.—Every point of the curve is equally distant from the focus and from the directrix.—Construction of the parabola.

The parabola may be considered as an ellipse, in which the major axis is indefinitely increased while the distance from one focus to the adjacent summit remains constant.

Equations of the tangent and of the normal.—Sub-tangent and sub-normal. They furnish means of drawing a tangent at any point of the curve.

The tangent makes equal angles with the axis and with the radius vector drawn to the point of contact.—To draw, by means of this property, a tangent to the parabola, 1° through a point on the curve; 2° through an exterior point.

All the diameters of the parabola are right lines parallel to the axis, and reciprocally.—The chords which a diameter bisects are parallel to the tangent drawn at the extremity of that diameter.

Expression of the area of a parabolic segment.

Polar co-ordinates.—To pass from a system of rectilinear and rectangular co-ordinates to a system of polar co-ordinates, and reciprocally.

Polar equations of the three curves of the second order, the pole being situated at a focus, and the angles being reckoned from the axis which passes through that focus.

Summary discussion of some transcendental curves.—Determination of the tangent at one of their points.

Construction of the real roots of equations of any form with one unknown quantity.—Investigation of the intersections of two curves of the second degree.—Numerical applications of these formulas.

* They will be deduced from the property, previously demonstrated, of the derivative of the ordinate with respect to the abscissa.

2. GEOMETRY OF THREE DIMENSIONS.

The sum of the projections of several consecutive right lines upon an axis is equal to the projection of the resulting line.—The sum of the projections of a right line on three rectangular axes is equal to the square of the right line.—The sum of the squares of the cosines of the angles which a right line makes with three rectangular right lines is equal to unity.

The projection of a plane area on a plane is equal to the product of that area by the cosine of the angle of the two planes.

Representation of a point by its co-ordinates.—Equations of lines and of surfaces.

Transformation of rectilinear co-ordinates.

Of the right line and of the plane.

Equations of the right line.—Equation of the plane.

To find the equations of a right line, 1° which passes through two given points, 2° which passes through a given point and which is parallel to a given line.

To determine the point of intersection of two right lines whose equations are known.

To pass a plane, 1° through three given points; 2° through a given point and parallel to a given plane; 3° through a point and through a given right line.

Knowing the equations of two planes, to find the projections of their intersection.

To find the intersection of a right line and of a plane, their equations being known.

Knowing the co-ordinates of two points, to find their distance.

From a given point to let fall a perpendicular on a plane; to find the foot and the length of that perpendicular (rectangular co-ordinates).

Through a given point to pass a plane perpendicular to a given right line (rectangular co-ordinates).

Through a given point, to pass a perpendicular to a given right line; to determine the foot and the length of that perpendicular (rectangular co-ordinates).

Knowing the equations of a right line, to determine the angles which that line makes with the axes of the co-ordinates (rectangular co-ordinates).

To find the angle of two right lines whose equations are known (rectangular co-ordinates).

Knowing the equation of a plane, to find the angles which it makes with the co-ordinate planes (rectangular co-ordinates).

To determine the angle of two planes (rectangular co-ordinates).

To find the angle of a right line and of a plane (rectangular co-ordinates).

Surfaces of the second degree.

They are divided into two classes; one class having a centre, the other not having any. Co-ordinates of the centre.

Of diametric planes.

Simplification of the general equation of the second degree by the transformation of co-ordinates.

The simplest equations of the ellipsoid, of the hyperboloid of one sheet and of two sheets, of the elliptical and the hyperbolic paraboloid, of cones and of cylinders of the second order.

Nature of the plane sections of surfaces of the second order.—Plane sections of the cone, and of the right cylinder with circular base.—Anti-parallel section of the oblique cone with circular base.

Cone asymptote to an hyperboloid.

Right-lined sections of the hyperboloid of one sheet.—Through each point of a hyperboloid of one sheet two right lines can be drawn, whence result two systems of right-lined generatrices of the hyperboloid.—Two right lines taken in the same system do not meet, and two right lines of different systems always meet.—All the right lines situated on the hyperboloid being transported to the centre, remaining parallel to themselves, coincide with the surface of the asymptote cone.—Three right lines of the same system are never parallel to the same plane.—The hyperboloid of one sheet may be generated by a right line which moves along three fixed right lines, not parallel to the same plane; and, reciprocally, when a right line slides on three fixed lines, not parallel to the same plane, it generates a hyperboloid of one sheet.

Right-lined sections of the hyperbolic paraboloid.—Through each point of the surface of the hyperbolic paraboloid two right lines may be traced, whence results the generation of the paraboloid by two systems of right lines.—Two right lines of the same system do not meet, but two right lines of different systems always meet.—All the right lines of the same system are parallel to the same plane.—The hyperbolic paraboloid may be generated by the movement of a right line which slides on three fixed right lines which are parallel to the same plane; or by a right line which slides on two fixed right lines, itself remaining always parallel to a given plane. Reciprocally, every surface resulting from one of these two modes of generation is a hyperbolic paraboloid.

General equations of conical surfaces and of cylindrical surfaces.

VI. DESCRIPTIVE GEOMETRY.

The general methods of Descriptive Geometry,—their uses in Stone-cutting and Carpentry, in Linear Perspective, and in the determination of the Shadows of bodies,—constitute one of the most fruitful branches of the applications of mathematics. The course has always been given at the Polytechnic School with particular care, according to the plans traced by the illustrious *Monge*, but no part of the subject has heretofore been required for admission. The time given to it in the school, being however complained of on all sides as insufficient for its great extent and important applications, the general methods of Descriptive Geometry will henceforth be retrenched from the internal course, and be required of all candidates for admission.

As to the programme itself, it is needless to say any thing, for it was established by *Monge*, and the extent which he gave to it, as well as the methods which he had created, have thus far been maintained. We merely suppress the construction of the shortest distance between two right lines, which presents a disagreeable and useless complication.

Candidates will have to present to the examiner a collection of their graphical constructions (*épures*) of all the questions of the programme, signed by their teacher. They are farther required to make free-hand sketches of five of their *épures*.

PROGRAMME OF DESCRIPTIVE GEOMETRY.

*Problems relating to the point, to the straight line, and to the plane.**

Through a point given in space, to pass a right line parallel to a given right line, and to find the length of a part of that right line.

Through a given point, to pass a plane parallel to a given plane.

To construct the plane which passes through three points given in space.

Two planes being given, to find the projections of their intersection.

A right line and a plane being given, to find the projections of the point in which the right line meets the plane.

Through a given point, to pass a perpendicular to a given plane, and to construct the projections of the point of meeting of the right line and of the plane.

Through a given point, to pass a right line perpendicular to a given right line, and to construct the projections of the point of meeting of the two right lines.

A plane being given, to find the angles which it forms with the planes of projection.

Two planes being given, to construct the angle which they form between them.

Two right lines which cut each other being given, to construct the angle which they form between them.

To construct the angle formed by a right line and by a plane given in position in space.

Problems relating to tangent planes.

To draw a plane tangent to a cylindrical surface or to a conical surface, 1° through a point taken on the surface; 2° through a point taken out of the surface; 3° parallel to a given right line.

Through a point taken on a surface of revolution, whose meridian is known, to pass a plane tangent to that surface.

---

* The method of the change of the planes of projection will be used for the resolution of these problems.

Problems relating to the intersection of surfaces.

To construct the section made, on the surface of a right and vertical cylinder, by a plane perpendicular to one of the planes of projection.—To draw the tangent to the curve of intersection.—To make the development of the cylindrical surface, and to refer to it the curve of intersection, and also the tangent.

To construct the intersection of a right cone by a plane perpendicular to one of the planes of projection. Development and tangent.

To construct the right section of an oblique cylinder.—To draw the tangent to the curve of intersection. To make the development of the cylindrical surface, and to refer to it the curve which served as its base, and also its tangents.

To construct the intersection of a surface of revolution by a plane, and the tangents to the curve of intersection.—To resolve this question, when the generating line is a right line which does not meet the axis.

To construct the intersection of two cylindrical surfaces, and the tangents to that curve.

To construct the intersection of two oblique cones, and the tangents to that curve.

To construct the intersection of two surfaces of revolution whose axes meet.

VII. OTHER REQUIREMENTS.

The preceding six heads complete the outline of the elementary course of mathematical instruction which it was the object of this article to present; but a few more lines may well be given to a mere enumeration of the other requirements for admission to the school.

MECHANICS comes next. The programme is arranged under these heads: Simple motion and compound motion; Inertia; Forces applied to a free material point; Work of forces applied to a movable point; Forces applied to a solid body; Machines.

PHYSICS comprises these topics: General properties of bodies; Hydrostatics and hydraulics; Densities of solids and liquids; Properties of gases; Heat; Steam; Electricity; Magnetism; Acoustics; Light.

CHEMISTRY treats of Oxygen; Hydrogen; Combinations of hydrogen with oxygen; Azote or nitrogen; Combinations of azote with oxygen; Combination of azote with hydrogen, or ammonia; Sulphur; Chlorine; Phosphorus; Carbon.

COSMOGRAPHY describes the Stars; the Earth; the Sun; the Moon; the Planets; Comets; the Tides.

HISTORY and GEOGRAPHY treat of Europe from the Roman Empire to the accession of Louis XVI.

GERMAN must be known sufficiently for it to be translated, spoken a little, and written in its own characters.

DRAWING, besides the *épures* of descriptive geometry, must have been acquired sufficiently for copying an academic study, and shading in pencil and in India ink.

Will not our readers agree with M. Coriolis, that "*There are very few learned mathematicians who could answer perfectly well at an examination for admission to the Polytechnic School*"?

SCHOOLS OF PREPARATION FOR THE POLYTECHNIC SCHOOL.

THERE are strictly speaking no Junior Military Schools preparatory to the Polytechnic School, or to the Special Military School at St. Cyr. These schools are recruited in general from the *Lycées* and other schools for secondary instruction, upon which they exert a most powerful influence. Until 1852 there was no special provision made in the courses of instruction in the *Lycées* for the mathematical preparation required for admission into the Polytechnic, and the Bachelor's degree in science could not be obtained without being able to meet the requirements in Latin, rhetoric, and logic for graduation in the arts, which was necessary to the profession of law, medicine, and theology. In consequence, young men who prepared to be candidates for the preliminary examinations at the Polytechnic and the St. Cyr, left the *Lycées* before graduation in order to acquire more geometry and less literature in the private schools, or under private tuition.

A new arrangement, popularly called the *Bifurcation*, was introduced by the Decrees of the 10th of April, 1852; and has now come into operation. The conditions demanded for the degree in science were adapted to the requirements of the Military Schools; and in return for this concession it is henceforth to be exacted from candidates for the Military Schools. The diploma of arts is no longer required before the diploma of science can be given. The instruction, which in the upper classes of the *Lycées* had hitherto been mainly preparatory for the former, takes henceforth at a certain point (called that of *Bifurcation*) two different routes, conducting separately, the one to the baccalaureate of arts, the other to that of science. The whole system of teaching has accordingly been altered. Boys wanting to study algebra are no longer carried through a long course of Latin; mathematics are raised to an equality with literature; and thus military pupils—pupils desirous of admission at the Polytechnic and St. Cyr, may henceforth, it is hoped, obtain in the *Lycées* all the preparation which they had latterly sought elsewhere.

Under this new system the usual course for a boy seems to be the following:—

He enters the *Lycée*, in the Elementary Classes; or, a little later, in the Grammar Classes, where he learns Latin and begins Greek. At the age of about fourteen, he is called upon to pass an examination for admission into the Upper Division, and here, in accordance with the new regulations, he makes his choice for mathematics or for literature, the studies henceforth being divided, one course leading to the bachelorship of science, the other to that of arts.

In either case he has before him three yearly courses, three classes—the Third, the Second, and what is called the Rhetoric. At the close of this, or after passing, if he pleases, another year in what is called the Logic, he may go up for his bachelor's degree. The boy who wants to go to St. Cyr or the Polytechnic chooses, of course, the mathematical division leading to the diploma he will want, that of a bachelor of *science*. He accordingly begins algebra, goes on to trigonometry, to conic sections, and to mechanics, and through corresponding stages in natural philosophy, and the like. If he chooses to spend a fourth year in the Logic, he will be chiefly employed in going over his subjects again. He may take his bachelor's degree at any time after finishing his third year; and he may, if he pleases, having taken that, remain during a fifth or even a sixth year, in the class of Special Mathematics.

If he be intended for St. Cyr, he may very well leave at the end of his year in Rhetoric, taking of course his degree. One year in the course of Special Mathematics will be required before he can have a chance for the Polytechnic. Usually the number of students admitted at the latter, who have not passed more than one year in the *mathematiques spéciales* is very small. Very probably the young aspirant would try at the end of his first year in this class, and would learn by practice to do better at the end of the second.

The following are the studies of the mathematical section of the upper division as laid down by the ordinance of 30th August, 1854.

THE THIRD CLASS (*Troisième*,) at fourteen years old.

Arithmetic and first notions of Algebra. Plane Geometry and its applications. First notions of Chemistry and Physics. General notions of Natural History; Principles of classification. Linear and imitative Drawing.

THE SECOND CLASS (*Seconde*,) at fifteen years old.

Algebra; Geometry, figures in space, recapitulation; Applications of Geometry, notions of the geometrical representations of bodies by projections; Rectilineal Trigonometry; Chemistry; Physics; and Drawing.

THE RHETORIC, at sixteen years old.

Exercises in Arithmetic and Algebra; Geometry; notions on some common curves; and general recapitulation; Applications of Geometry; notions of leveling and its processes; recapitulation of Trigonometry; Cosmography; Mechanics; Chemistry concluded and reviewed; Zoölogy and Animal Physiology; Botany and Vegetable Physiology; Geology; Drawing. (The pupil may now be ready for the Degree and for St. Cyr.)

THE LOGIC, at seventeen years old.

Six lessons a week are employed in preparation for the bachelorship of science, and in a methodical recapitulation of the courses of the three preceding years according to the state of the pupil's knowledge.

Two lessons a week are allowed for reviewing the literary instruction; evening lessons in Latin, French, English, and German, and in History and Geography, having been given through the whole previous time.

THE SPECIAL MATHEMATICS, at eighteen and nineteen years old.

Five lessons a week are devoted to these studies; in the other lessons the pupils join those of the Logic class for reviewing all their previous subjects, whether for the bachelorship in science or for competition for admission at the *Ecole Normale* or the Polytechnic.

It will only be necessary to add a few sentences in explanation of the methods pursued in the upper classes of the *Lycées.* The classes are large—from 80 to above 100; the lessons strictly professorial lectures, with occasional questions, as at the Polytechnic itself. In large establishments the class is divided, and two professors are employed, giving two parallel courses on the same subject. To correct and fortify this general teaching, we find, corresponding to the interrogations of the Polytechnic, what are here called conferences. The members of the large class are examined first of all in small detachments of five or six by their own professors once a week; and, secondly, a matter of yet greater importance, by the professor who is conducting the parallel course, and by professors who are engaged for this purpose from other *Lycées* and preparatory schools, and from among the *répétiteurs* of the Polytechnic and the Ecole Normale themselves. It appeared by the table of the examinations of this latter kind which had been passed by the pupils of the class of Special Mathematics at the *Lycée* St. Louis, that the first pupil on the list had in the interval between the opening of the school and the date of our visit (February 16th) gone through as many as twenty-four.

The assistants, who bear the name of *répétiteurs* at the *Lycées*, do not correspond in any sense to those whom we shall hereafter notice at the Ecole Polytechnique. They are in the *Lycées* mere superintendents in the *salles d'étude*, who attend to order and discipline, who give some slight occasional help to the pupils, and may be employed in certain cases, where the parents wish for it, in giving private tuition to the less proficient. The system of *salles d'étude* appears to prevail universally; the number of the pupils placed in each probably varying greatly. At the Polytechnic we found eight or ten pupils in each; at St. Cyr as many as 200. The number considered most desirable at the *Lycée* of St. Louis was stated to be thirty.

It thus appears that in France not only do private establishments succeed in giving preparation for the military schools, but that even in the first-class public schools, which educate for the learned professions, it has been considered possible to conduct a series of military or science classes by the side of the usual literary or arts classes. The common upper schools are not, as they used to be, and as with us they are, *Grammar* schools, they are also *Science* schools. In every *Lycée* there is, so to say, a sort of elementary polytechnic department, giving a kind of instruction which will be useful to the future soldier, and at the same time to others, to those who may have to do with mines, manufactures, or any description of civil engineering. There is thus no occasion for Junior Military Schools in France, for all the schools of this class are more or less of a military character in their studies.

The conditions of admission to the examination for the degree of Bachelor of Science are simply, sixteen years of age, and the payment of fees amounting to about 200 fr. (10*l.*) Examinations are held three times a year by the Faculties at Paris, Besançon, Bordeaux, Caen, Clermont, Dijon, Grenoble, Lille, Lyons, Marseilles, Montpellier, Nancy, Poitiers, Rennes, Strasburg, and Toulouse, and once a year at Ajaccio, Algiers, and nineteen other towns. There is a written examination of six hours, and a vivâ voce examination of an hour and a quarter. It is, of course, only a *pass* examination, and is said to be much less difficult than the competitive examination for admission to St. Cyr.—*Report of English Commissioners*, 1856.

THE POLYTECHNIC SCHOOL OF FRANCE.

CONTENTS.

THE POLYTECHNIC SCHOOL AT PARIS.*

I. FOUNDATION AND HISTORY.

THE origin of the *Ecole Polytechnique* dates from a period of disorder and distress in the history of France which might seem alien to all intellectual pursuits, if we did not remember that the general stimulus of a revolutionary period often acts powerfully upon thought and education. It is, perhaps, even more than the Institute, the chief scientic creation of the first French Revolution. It was during the government of the committee of public safety, when Carnot, as war minister, was gradually driving back the invading armies, and reorganizing victory out of defeat and confusion, that the first steps were taken for its establishment. A law, dating the 1st Ventose, year II., the 12th of March 1794, created a "Commission des Travaux Publics," charged with the duty of establishing a regular system for carrying on public works; and this commission ultimately founded a central school for public works, and drew up a plan for the competitive examination of candidates for admission to the service. It was intended at first to give a complete education for some of the public services, but it was soon changed into a preparatory school, to be succeeded by special schools of application. This was the Ecole Polytechnique.

The school and its plan were both owing to an immediate and pressing want. It was to be partly military and partly civil. Military, as well as civil education had been destroyed by the revolutionists. The committee of public safety had, indeed, formed a provisional school for engineers at Metz, to supply the immediate wants of the army on the frontier, and at this school young men were hastily taught the elements of fortification, and were sent direct to the troops, to learn as they best could, the practice of their art. "But such a method," says the report accompanying the law which founded the school, "does not form engineers *in any true sense of the term*, and can only be justified by the emergency of the

* Compiled from "*Report and Appendix of English Commissioners on Military Education.*" 1857.

time. The young men should be recalled to the new school to complete their studies." Indeed no one knew better than Carnot, to use the language of the report, "that patriotism and courage can not "always supply the want of knowledge;" and in the critical campaigns of 1793—4, he must often have felt the need of the institution which he was then contributing to set on foot. Such was the immediate motive for the creation of this school. At first, it only included the engineers amongst its pupils. But the artillery were added within a year.

We must not, however, omit to notice its civil character, the combination of which with its military object forms its peculiar feature, and has greatly contributed to its reputation. Amongst its founders were men, who though ardent revolutionists, were thirsting for the restoration of schools and learning, which for a time had been totally extinguished. The chief of these, besides Carnot, were Monge and Fourcroy, Berthollet and Lagrange. Of Carnot and Lagrange, one amongst the first of war ministers, the other one of the greatest of mathematicians, we need not say more. Berthollet, a man of science and practical skill, first suggested the school; Monge, the founder of Descriptive Geometry, a favorite *savant* of Napoleon though a zealous republican, united to real genius that passion for teaching and for his pupils, which makes the *beau idéal* of the founder of a school; and Fourcroy was a man of equal practical tact and science, who at the time had great influence with the convention, and was afterwards intrusted by Napoleon with much of the reorganization of education in France.

When the school first started there was scarcely another of any description in the country. For nearly three years the revolution had destroyed every kind of teaching. The attack upon the old schools, in France, as elsewhere, chiefly in the hands of the clergy, had been begun by a famous report of Talleyrand's, presented to the legislative assembly in 1791, which recommended to suppress all the existing academies within Paris and the provinces, and to replace them by an entirely new system of national education through the country. In this plan a considerable number of military schools were proposed, where boys were to be educated from a very early age. When the violent revolutionists were in power, they adopted the destructive part of Talleyrand's suggestions without the other. All schools, from the university downwards, were destroyed; the large exhibitions or *Bourses*, numbering nearly 40,000, were confiscated or plundered by individuals, and even the military schools and those for the public works (which were absolutely necessary for the very roads and the defense of the country) were suppressed or disorganized. The school of engineers at Mézières (an excellent one, where Monge had been a professor,) and that of the artillery at La Fère, were both broken up, whilst the murder of Lavoisier, and the well known saying in respect to it, that "the Republic had no need of chemists," gave currency to a belief, which Fourcroy expressed in proposing the Polytechnic, "that the late conspirators had formed a deliberate plan to destroy the arts and sciences, and to establish their tyranny on the ruins of human reason."

Thus it was on the ruin of all the old teaching, that the new institution was erected; a truly *revolutionary* school, as its founders delighted to call it, using the term as it was then commonly used, as a synonym for all that was excellent. And then for the first time avowing the principle of public competition, its founders, Monge and Fourcroy, began their work with an energy and enthusiasm which they seem to have left as a traditional inheritance to their school. It is curious to see the difficulties which the bankruptcy of the country threw in their way, and the vigor with which, assisted by the summary powers of the republican government, they overcame them. They begged the old Palais Bourbon for their building; were supplied with pictures from the Louvre; the fortunate capture of an English ship gave them some uncut diamonds for their first experiments; presents of military instruments were sent from the arsenals of Havre; and even the hospitals contributed some chemical substances In fine, having set their school in motion, the government and its professors worked at it with such zeal and effect, that within five months after their project was announced, they had held their first entrance examination, open to the competition of all France, and started with three hundred and seventy-nine pupils.

The account of one of these first pupils, who is among the most distinguished still surviving ornaments of the Polytechnic, will convey a far better idea of the spirit of the young institution than could be given by a more lengthy description. M. Biot described to us vividly the zeal of the earliest teachers, and the thirst for knowledge which, repressed for awhile by the horrors of the period, burst forth with fresh ardor amongst the French youth of the time. Many of them, he said, like himself, had been carried away by the enthusiasm of the revolution, and had entered the army. "My father had sent me," he added, "to a mercantile house, and indeed I never felt any great vocation to be a soldier, but *Que voulez vous?*

les Prussiens etaient en Champagne." He joined the army, served two years under Dumouriez, and returned to Paris in the reign of terror, " to see from his lodgings in the Rue St. Honore the very generals who had led us to victory, Custine and Biron, carried by in the carts to the guillotine. " Imagine what it was when we heard that Robespierre was dead, and that we might return safely to study after all this misery, and then to have for our teachers La Place, Lagrange, and Monge. We felt like men brought to life again after suffocation. Lagrange said, modestly, "Let me teach them arithmetic." Monge was more like our father than our teacher; he would come to us in the evening, and assist us in our work till midnight, and when he explained a difficulty to one of our *chefs de brigade*, it ran like an electric spark through the party." The pupils were not then, he told us, as they have since been, shut up in barracks, they were left free, but there was no idleness or dissipation amongst them. They were united in zealous work and in good *camaraderie*, and any one known as a bad character was avoided. This account may be a little tinged by enthusiastic recollections, but it agreed almost entirely with that of M. de Barante, who bore similar testimony to the early devotion of the pupils, and the unique excellence of the teaching of Monge.

We are not, however, writing a history of this school, and must confine ourselves to such points as directly illustrate its system of teaching and its organization. These may be roughly enumerated in the following order:

1. Its early history is completed by the law of its organization, given it by La Place in his short ministry of the interior. This occurred in the last month of 1799, a memorable era in French history, for it was immediately after the revolution of the 18th of Brumaire, when Napoleon overthrew the Directory and made himself First Consul. One of his earliest acts was to sign the charter of his great civil and military school. This charter or decree deserves some attention, because it is always referred to as the law of the foundation of the school. It determined the composition of the two councils of instruction and improvement, the bodies to which the direction of the school was to be, and still is, intrusted; some of its marked peculiarities in the mode and subject of teaching. It is important to notice each of the two points.

The direction of the school was at first almost entirely in the hands of its professors, who formed what is still called its Council of Instruction. Each of them presided over the school alternately for one month, a plan copied from the revolutionary government of the Convention. In the course of a few years, however, another body was added, which has now the real management of the school. This is called the "Council of Improvement" (*Conseil de perfectionnement,*) and a part of its business is to see that the studies form a good preparation for those of the more special schools (*écoles d'application*) for the civil and military service. It consists of eminent men belonging to the various public departments supplied by the school, and some of the professors. It has had, as far as we could judge, an useful influence; *first*, as a body not liable to be prejudiced in its proposals by the feelings of the school, and yet interested in its welfare and understanding it; *secondly*, as having shown much skill in the difficult task of making the theoretical teaching of the Polytechnic a good introduction to the practical studies of the public service; *thirdly*, as being sufficiently influential, from the character of its members, to shield the school from occasional ill-judged interference. It should be added that hardly any year has passed without the Council making a full report on the studies of the school, with particular reference to their bearing on the Special Schools of Application.

The method of scientific teaching has been peculiar from the beginning. It is the most energetic form of what may be called the *repetitorial* system, a method of teaching almost peculiar to France, and which may be described as a very able combination of professional and tutorial teaching. The object of the *répétiteur*, or private tutor, is to second every lecture of the professor, to explain and fix it by ocular demonstration, explanations, or examination. This was a peculiarity in the scheme of Monge and Fourcroy. The latter said, in the first programme, "Our pupils must not only learn, they must at once carry out their theory. We must distribute them into small rooms, where they shall practice the plans of descriptive geometry, which the professors have just shown them in their public lectures. And in the same manner they must go over in practice (*répéteront*) in separate laboratories the principal operations of chemistry." To carry out this system the twenty best pupils, of whom M. Biot was one, were selected as *répétiteurs* soon after the school had started. Since then the vacancies have always been filled by young but competent men, aspiring themselves to become in turn professors. They form a class of teachers more like the highest style of private tutors in our universities, or what are called in Germany *Privat-docenten*, than any other body—with this difference, that they do not give their own lectures, but breaking up the professor's large class into small classes of five and six pupils, examine these in *his* lecture. The success of this attempt we shall de scribe hereafter.

2. A change may be noticed which was effected very early by the Council of Improvement—the union of pupils for artillery and engineers in a single school of application. The first report in December 1800, speaks of the identity in extent and character of the studies required for these two services; and in conformity with its recommendation, the law of the 3rd of October 1802, (12th Vendémiaire, XI.) dissolved the separate artillery school at Châlons, and established the united school for both arms in the form which it still retains at Metz.

3. In 1805 a curious change was made, and one very characteristic of the school. The pupils have always been somewhat turbulent, and generally on the side of opposition. In the earliest times they were constantly charged with *incivisme*, and the aristocracy was said to have "taken refuge within its walls." In fact, one of its earliest and of its few great *literary* pupils, M. de Barante, confirmed this statement, adding, as a reason, that the school gave for a while the only good instruction in France. It was in consequence of some of these changes that the pupils who had hitherto lived in their own private houses or lodgings in Paris, were collected in the school building. This "*casernement*," said to be immediately owing to a burst of anger of Napoleon, naturally tended to give the school a more military character; but it was regarded as an unfortunate change by its chief scientific friends. "*Ah! ma pauvre école!*" M. Biot told us he had exclaimed, when he saw their knapsacks on their beds. He felt, he said, that the enthusiasm of free study was gone, and that now they would chiefly work by routine and compulsion.

4. The year 1809 may be called the epoch at which the school attained its final character. By this time the functions, both of boards and teachers, were accurately fixed, some alterations in the studies had taken place, and the plan of a final examination had been drawn up, according to which the pupils were to obtain their choice of the branch of the public service they preferred. In fact, the school may be said to have preserved ever since the form it then assumed, under a variety of governments and through various revolutions, in most of which, indeed, its pupils have borne some share; and one of which, the restoration of 1816, was attended with its temporary dissolution.

Thus, during the first years after its foundation the Polytechnic grew and flourished in the general dearth of public teaching, being indeed not merely the only great school, but, until the Institute was founded, the only scientific body in France. Working on its first idea of high professorial lectures, practically applied and explained by *répétiteurs*, its success in its own purely scientific line was, and has continued to be, astonishing. Out of its sixteen earliest professors, ten still retain an European name. Lagrange, Monge, Fourcroy, La Place, Guyton de Morveau were connected with it. Malus, Hauy, Biot, Poisson, and De Barante, were among its earliest pupils. Arago, Cauchy, Cavaignac, Lamoricière, with many more modern names, came later. All the great engineers and artillerymen of the empire belonged to it, and the long pages in its calendar of distinguished men are the measure of its influence on the civil and military services of France. In fact its pupils, at a time of enormous demands, supplied all the scientific offices of the army, and directed all the chief public works, fortresses, arsenals, the improvement of cities, the great lines of roads, shipbuilding, mining—carried out, in a word, most of the great improvements of Napoleon. He knew the value of his school, "the hen" as he called it, "that laid him golden eggs"—and perhaps its young pupils were not improved by the excessive official patronage bestowed by him upon "the envy of Europe," "the first school in the world." It can not, however, be matter of surprise, that its vigor and success should have caused Frenchmen, even those who criticise its influence severely, to regard it with pride as an institution unrivaled for scientific purposes.

It is not necessary to give any detailed account of the later history of the school, but we must remark that disputes have frequently arisen with regard to the best mode of harmonizing its teaching with that of the special schools of application to which it conducts. These disputes have been no doubt increased by the union of a civil and military object in the same school. The scientific teaching desirable for some of the higher civil professions has appeared of doubtful advantage to those destined for the more practical work of war. There has been always a desire on the one side to qualify pure mathematics by application, a strong feeling on the other that mathematical study sharpens the mind most keenly for some of the practical pursuits of after life. We should add, perhaps, that there has been some protest in France (though little heard among the scientific men who have been the chief directors of the school) against the *esprit faux*, the exclusive pursuit of mathematics to the utter neglect of literature, and the indifference to moral and historical studies. Some one or other of these complaints any one who studies the *literature*, the pamphlets, and history of the school will find often reproduced in the letters of war ministers, of artillery and engineer officers commanding the school of application at Metz, or of committees from the similar schools for the mines and the roads and bridges. The last of these occasions illustrates the present position of the school.

On the 5th of June 1850, the legislative assembly appointed a mixed commission of military men and civilians, who were charged to revise all the programs of instruction, and to recommend all needful changes in the studies of the pupils, both those preparatory to entrance* and those actually pursued in the school. The commission was composed as follows :—

M. Thenard, Member of the Academy of Sciences, and of the Board of Improvement of the Polytechnic School, President.

Le Verrier, Member of the Academy of Sciences and of the Legislative Assembly, Reporter.

Noizet, General of Brigade of Engineers.

Poncelet, General of Brigade of Engineers, Commandant of the Polytechnic School, Member of the Academy of Sciences.

Piobert, General of Brigade of Artillery, Member of the Academy of Sciences.

Mathieu, Rear Admiral.

Duhamel, Member of the Academy of Sciences, Director of Studies at the Polytechnic School.

Mary, Divisional Inspector of Roads and Bridges.

Morin, Colonel of Artillery, Member of the Academy of Sciences.

Regnault, Engineer of Mines, Member of the Academy of Sciences.

Olivier, Professor at the *Conservatoire des Arts et Metiers.*

Debacq, Secretary for Military Schools at the Ministry of War, Secretary.

A chronic dispute which has gone on from the very first year of the school's existence, between the exclusive study of abstract mathematics on the one hand, and their early practical application on the other, was brought to a head (though it has scarcely been set at rest) by this commission. All the alterations effected have been in the direction of eliminating a portion of the pure mathematics, and of reducing abstract study to the limits within which it was believed to be most directly applicable to practice. The results, however, are still a subject of vehement dispute, in which most of the old scientific pupils of the Polytechnic, and many of what may be styled its most practical members, the officers of the artillery and engineers, are ranged on the side of "early and deep scientific study *versus* early practical applications." It is, indeed, a question which touches the military pupils nearly, since it is in their case particularly that the proposed abstract studies of the Polytechnic might be thought of the most doubtful advantage. We do not try to solve the problem here, though the facts elsewhere stated will afford some materials for judgment. We incline to the opin-

* In an Analysis of the Report of this Commission, see page 97.

ion of those who think that the ancient *genius loci*, the traditional teaching of the school, will be too strong for legislative interference, and that, in spite of recent enactments, abstract science and analysis will reign in the lecture-rooms and halls of study of the Polytechnic, now as in the days of Monge.

II. AN OUTLINE OF THE MANAGEMENT AND OF THE ESTABLISHMENT OF THE SCHOOL, ETC.

The Polytechnic, as we have said, is a preparatory and general scientific school; its studies are not exclusively adapted for any one of the departments to which at the close of its course the scholars will find themselves assigned; and on quitting it they have, before entering on the actual discharge of their duties of whatever kind, to pass through a further term of teaching in some one of the schools of application specially devoted to particular professions.

The public services for which it thus gives a general preparation are the following:

Military: Under the Minister at War.

Artillery (*Artillerie de terre.*)
Engineers (*Génie.*)
The Staff Corps (*Corps d'Etat Major.*)
The Department of Powder and Saltpetre (*Poudres et Salpêtres.*)

Under the Minister of Marine.

Navy, (*Marine.*)
Marine Artillery (*Artillerie de mer.*)
Naval Architects (*Génie maritime.*)
The Hydrographical Department (*Corps des Ingénieurs Hydrographes.*)

Civil: Under the Minister of Public Works.

The Department of Roads and Bridges (*Ponts-et-chaussées.*)
The Department of Mines (*Mines.*)

Under the Minister of the Interior.

The Telegraph Department (*Lignes Télégraphiques.*)

Under the minister of Finance.

The Tobacco Department (*Administration des Tabacs.*)

To these may be added at any time, by a decree on the part of the government, any other departments, the duties of which appear to require an extensive knowledge of mathematics, physics, or chemistry.

Admission to the school is, and has been since its first commencement in 1794, obtained by competition in a general examination, held yearly, and open to all. Every French youth, between the age of sixteen and twenty, (or if in the army up to the age of twenty-five,) may offer himself as a candidate.

A board of examiners passes through France once every year, and examines all who present themselves, that have complied with the conditions, which are fully detailed in the decree given in the appendix. It commences at Paris.

A list of such of the candidates as are found eligible for admittance to the Polytechnic is drawn up from the proceedings of the board, and submitted to the minister at war; the number of places likely to be vacant has already been determined, and the minister fixes the number of admissions accordingly. The candidates admitted are invariably taken in the order of merit.

The annual charge for board and instruction is 40*l.* (1,000 fr.,) payable in advance in four installments. In addition there is the cost of outfit, varying from 20*l.* to 24*l.* Exhibitions, however, for the discharge of the whole or of one-half of the expense (*bourses* and *demi-bourses*,) are awarded by the state in favor of *all* the successful candidates, whose parents can prove themselves to be too poor to maintain their children in the school. Outfits and half outfits (*trousseaux*) and *demi-trousseaux*) are also granted in these cases, on the entrance of the student into the school; and the number of these *boursiers* and *demi-boursiers* amounts at the present time to one-third of the whole.

The course of study is completed in two years. On its successful termination which is preceded by a final examination, the students are distributed into the different services, the choice being offered them in the order of their merit, and laid down in the classified list drawn up after the examination. If it so happen that the number of places or the services which can be offered is not sufficient for the number of qualified students, those at the bottom of the list are offered service in the infantry or cavalry, and those who do not enter the public service, are supplied with certificates of having passed successfully through the school. Students who have been admitted into the school from the army, are abliged to re-enter the army.

All others, as has been said, have the right of choosing, according to their position on the list, the service which they prefer, so far, that is, as the number of vacancies in that service will allow; or they may if they please decline to enter the public service at all.

Such is a general outline of the plan and object of the school. We may add that, besides its military staff, it employs no less than thirty-nine professors and teachers; that it has four boards of management, and that ten scientific men unconnected with the school, and amongst the most distinguished in France, conduct its examinations. The magnitude of this establishment for teaching may be estimated by the fact, that the number of pupils rarely exceeds three hundred and fifty, and is often much less.

A fuller enumeration of these bodies will complete our present sketch.

I. The military establishment consists of:—

The Commandant, a General Officer, usually of the Artillery or the Engineers, at present a General of Artillery.

A Second in Command, a Colonel or Lieutenant-Colonel, chosen from former pupils of school; at present a Colonel of Engineers.

Three Captains of Artillery and Three Captains of Engineers, as Inspectors of Studies, chosen also from former pupils of the school.

Six Adjutants (*adjoints*,) non-commissioned officers, usually such as have been recommended for promotion.

II. The civil establishment consists of:—

1. A Director of Studies, who has generally been a civilian, but is at present a Lieutenant-Colonel of Engineers.

2. Fifteen Professors, viz.:—Two of Mathematical Analysis. Two of Mechanics and Machinery. One of Descriptive Geometry. Two of Physics. Two of Chemistry. One of Military Art and Fortification. One of Geodesy. One of Architecture. One of French Composition. One of German. One of Drawing. Of these one is an officer of the Staff, another of the Artillery, and a third of the Navy; two are Engineers in Chief of the Roads and Bridges; nine are civilians, of whom two are Members of the Academy of Sciences.

3. Three Drawing Masters for Landscape and Figure Drawing; one for Machine Drawing, and one for Topographical Drawing.

4. Nineteen Assistant and Extra Assistant Teachers, (*répétiteurs* and *répétiteurs adjoints*) whose name and functions are both peculiar.

5. Five Examiners for Admission, consisting at present of one Colonel of Artillery, as President, and four civilians.

6. Five Examiners of Students (civilians,) four of them belonging to the Academy of Sciences.

7. There is also a separate Department for the ordinary Management of Administration of the affairs of the school, the charge of the fabric and of the library and museums; and a Medical Staff.

III. The general control or supervision of the school is vested, under the war department, in four great boards of councils, viz.:—

1. A board of administration, composed of the commandant, the second in command, the director of studies, two professors, two captains, and two members of the administrative staff. This board has the superintendence of all the financial business and all the minutiæ of the internal administration of the school.

2. A board of discipline, consisting of the second in command, the director, two professors, three captains (of the school,) and two captains of the army, chosen from former pupils. The duty of this board is to decide upon cases of misconduct.

3. A board of instruction, whose members are, the commandant, the second in command, the director, the examiners of students, and the professors; and whose chief duty is to make recommendations relating to ameliorations in the studies, the programmes of admission and of instruction in the school, to—

4. A board of improvement, charged with the general control of the studies, formed of—

The Commandant, as President.
The Second in Command.
The Director of Studies.
Two Delegates from the Department of Public Works.
One Delegate from the Naval Department.
One Delegate from the Home Department.
Three Delegates from the War Department.
Two Delegates from the Academy of Sciences.
Two Examiners of Students.
Three Professors of the School.

III. CONDITIONS AND EXAMINATIONS FOR ADMISSION.

The entrance examination is held yearly in August; the most important conditions for admission to it are always inserted in the *Moniteur* early in the year, and are—

1st. All candidates must be bachelors of science.

2nd. All candidates (unless they have served in the army) must have been as much as sixteen and not more than twenty years old on the 1st of January preceding.

3rd. Privates and non-commissioned officers of the army must be above twenty and under twenty-five years of age; must have served two years, and have certificates of good conduct.

4th. Candidates who propose to claim pecuniary assistance (a *bourse* or *demi-bourse*) must present formal proofs of their need of it.

The subjects of the entrance examination are the following:—

Arithmetic, including Vulgar and Decimal Fractions, Weights and Measures, Involution and Evolution; Simple Interest.

Geometry of Planes and Solids; application of Geometry to Surveying; Properties of Spherical Triangles.

Algebra, including Quadratic Equations with one unknown quantity, Series and Progressions in general; Binomial Theorem and its applications; Logarithms and their use; on Derived Functions; on the Theory of Equations; on Differences; application of the Theory of Differences to the Numerical Solution of Equations.

Plane and Spherical Trigonometry; Solution of Triangles; application of Trigonometry to Surveying.

Analytical Geometry, including Geometry of two dimensions; Co-ordinates; Equations of the first and second degree, with two variables; Tangents and Asymptotes; on the Ellipse, Hyperbola, and Parabola; Polar Co-ordinates; Curved Lines in general.

Geometry of three dimensions, including the Theory of Projections; Co-ordinates; the Right Line and Plane; Surfaces of the second degree; Conical and Cylindrical Surfaces.

Descriptive Geometry; Problems relative to a Point, Right Line and Plane; Tangent Planes; Intersection of Surfaces.

Mechanics; on the Movement of a Point considered geometrically; on the Effect of Forces applied to points and bodies at rest and moving; on the Mechanical Powers.

Natural Philosophy, including the Equilibrium of Liquids and Gasses; Heat;

Electricity; Magnetism; Galvanism; Electro-magnetism and Light; Cosmography.

Chemistry, the Elements; *French*; *German*; *Drawing*, and (optionally) *Latin*.

This examination is partly written and partly oral. It is not public, but conducted in the following manner:—

Five examiners are appointed by the minister of war to examine the candidates at Paris, and at the several towns named for the purpose throughout France.

Two of these examiners conduct what may be called a preliminary examination (*du premier degré*,) and the other three a second examination (*du second degré*.) The preliminary examiners precede by a few days in their journey through France those who conduct the second examination. The written compositions come before either.

The preliminary examination (*du premier degré*) is made solely for the purpose of ascertaining whether the candidates possess sufficient knowledge to warrant their being admitted to the second examination; and the second examination serves, in conjunction with the written compositions, for their classification in the order of merit.

Prior to the examination, each candidate is called upon to give in certain written sheets containing calculations, sketches, plans and drawings, executed by him at school during the year, certified and dated by the professor under whom he has studied. Care is taken to ascertain whether these are the pupils' own work, and any deception in this matter, if discovered, excludes at once from the competition of the school.

This done, the candidates are required to reply in writing to written or printed questions, and to write out French and German exercises; great care being taken to prevent copying. This written examination occupies about twenty-four hours during three and a half separate days, as shown in the following table. It usually takes place in the presence of certain official authorities, the examiners not being present.

First Sitting.	Hours.	*Second Sitting.*	Hours.
Arithmetic,	1	Algebra,	1
Geometry,	1	History, geography, and French,	3
Latin,	1		
	3		4
Third Sitting.		*Fourth Sitting.*	
Descriptive geometry, and diagram, or sketch,	4	Mechanics,	1
		Physics, chemistry, and cosmography,	2
			3

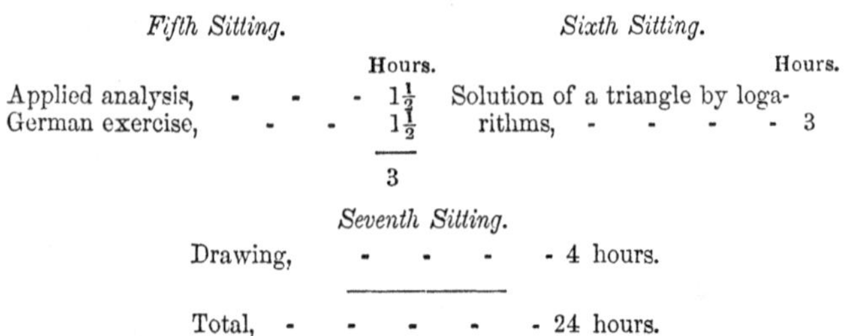

Fifth Sitting.	Hours.	*Sixth Sitting.*	Hours.
Applied analysis, - - -	$1\frac{1}{2}$	Solution of a triangle by logarithms, - - - -	3
German exercise, - -	$1\frac{1}{2}$		
	3		

Seventh Sitting.

Drawing, - - - -	4 hours.
Total, - - - - -	24 hours.

Next, each candidate is examined orally for three-quarters of an hour, on two successive days, by each of the two examiners separately, and each examiner makes a note of the admissibility or non-admissibility of the candidate.

At the close of this oral examination, the notes relating to the various candidates are compared, and if the examiners differ as to the admissibility of any candidate, he is recalled, further orally examined, and his written exercises carefully referred to, both examiners being present. A final decision is then made.

The preliminary examiners then supply the others with a list of the candidates who are entitled to be admitted to the second oral examination. On this occasion each candidate is separately examined for one hour and a half by each examiner, but care is taken that in all the principal subjects of study the candidate is examined by at least two out of the three examiners.

Each examiner records his opinion of the merits of every candidate in replying, orally and in writing, by awarding him a credit varying between 0 and 20, the highest number indicating a very superior result.

This scale of merit is employed to express the value of the oral replies, written answers, or drawings. It has the following signification, and appears to be generally in use in the French military schools:—

Credit	Signification	Credit	Signification
20	denotes perfect.	8, 7, 6	denotes bad.
19, 18	" very good.	5, 4, 3	" very bad.
17, 16, 15	" good.	2, 1	" almost nothing.
14, 13, 12	" passable.	0	" nothing.
11, 10, 9	" middling		

Considerable latitude is granted to the examiner engaged in deciding upon the amount of credit to be allowed to the student, for the manner in which he replies to the various questions. He is expected to bear in mind the temperament of the candidate, his confidence or timidity, as well as the difficulty of the questions, when judging of the quality of the reply, more value being given for an imperfect answer to a difficult question than for a more perfect reply to an easy one.

The reports of the examiners, together with the various documents belonging to each candidate, are sent from each town to the minister at war, who transmits them to the commandant of the Polytechnic School to make out a classified list.

Very different value of course is attached to the importance of some of the subjects, when compared with others; and the measure of the importance is represented in French examinations by what are termed *co-efficients of influence*, varying for the several subjects of study and kind of examination. The particular co-efficients of influence for each subject in these written and oral examinations, are as follows:—

	Co-efficients of Influence.	
Oral examination—analytical mathematics,	20	52
" " geometrical ditto,	14	
" " physics and mechanics,	16	
" " German language,	2	
Written compositions on mathematical subjects,	5	34
" " descriptive geometry, drawing, and description,	5	
" " logarithmic calculations of a triangle,	2	
" " mechanics,	2	
" " physics or chemistry,	4	
German exercise,	1	
French composition,	5	
Latin translation,	5	
Copy of a drawing,	5	
Total,		86

In order to make out the above mentioned classified list, the respective credits awarded by the examiners to each candidate are multiplied by the co-efficients representing the weight or importance attached to each subject; and the sum of their products furnishes a numerical result, representing the degree of merit of each candidate.

A comparison of these numerical results is then made, and a general list of all the candidates is arranged in order of merit.

This list, and the whole of the documents from which it has been drawn up, are then submitted to a jury composed of the

Commandant of the School.
The Second in Command.
The Director of Studies.
Two Members of the Board of Improvement.
The Five Examiners.

It is the special business of this jury carefully to scrutinize the whole of the candidates' documents, drawings, &c., and they further take care that a failure in any one branch of study is duly noted, as such failure is a sufficient reason for the exclusion of the candidate from the general list.

As soon as this general list has been thoroughly verified, it is submitted to the minister of war, who is empowered to add one-tenth to the number actually required for the public services; and thus it may happen that one-tenth of the pupils may annually be disappointed.

IV. THE SCHOOL BUILDINGS AND THE COURSE AND METHOD OF STUDY.

A brief description of the buildings may be a suitable introduction to an account of the studies that are pursued, and the life that is lead in them.

The Polytechnic School stands near the Pantheon, and consists of two main buildings, one for the official rooms and the residence of the commandant and director of. studies, the other, and larger one, for the pupils. Detached buildings contain the chemical lecture room and laboratory, the laboratory of natural philosophy, the library, fencing and billiard rooms.

The basement floor of the larger building contains the kitchen and refectories. On the first floor, are the two amphitheaters or great lecture rooms, assigned respectively to the pupils of the two years or divisions, in which the ordinary lectures are given. The rooms are large and well arranged; the seats fixed, the students' names attached to them. The students are admitted by doors behind the upper tier of seats; at the foot of all is a platform for the professor, with a blackboard facing his audience, and with sufficient room for a pupil to stand and work questions beside him. Room also is provided for one of the captains, inspectors of studies, whose duty it is to be present, for the director of studies, whose occasional presence is expected, and for the assistant teachers or *répétiteurs*, who in the first year of their appointment are called upon to attend the course upon which they will have to give their subsequent questions and explanations. On this floor are also the museums, or repositories of models, instruments, machines, &c., needed for use in the amphi theaters, or elsewhere. The museum provided for the lecturer on Physics (or Natural Philosophy) appeared in particular to be well supplied.

The whole of the second floor is taken up with what are called the *salles d'interrogation*, a long series of small cabinets or studies, plainly furnished with six or eight stools and a table, devoted to the *interrogations particulières*, which will presently be described.

The third floor contains the halls of study, *salles d'étude*, or studying rooms, in which the greater part of the student's time during the day is passed—where he studies, draws, keeps his papers and instruments, writes his exercises, and prepares his lectures. These are small chambers, containing eight or, exceptionally, eleven occupants. A double desk runs down the middle from the window to the door, with a little shelf and drawers for each student. There is a blackboard for the common use, and various objects are furnished through the senior student, the sergeant, a selected pupil, more advanced than the rest, who is placed in charge of the room, and is responsible for whatever is handed in for the use of the students. He collects the exercises, and generally gives a great deal of assistance to the less proficient. "When I was sergeant," said an old pupil, "I was always at the board." The spirit of *camaraderie*, said to exist so strongly among the Polytechnic students, displays itself in this particular form very beneficially. Young men of all classes work heartily and zealously togethen in the *salles d'étude*, and no feeling of rivalry prevents them from assisting one another. The sergeant does not, however, appear to exercise any authority in the way of keeping discipline.

These chambers for study are arranged on each side of a long corridor which runs through the whole length of the building, those of the juniors being separated from those of the seniors by a central chamber or compartment, the *cabinet de service*, where the officers charged with the discipline are posted, and from hence pass up and down the corridor, looking in through the glass doors and seeing that no interruption to order takes place.

The fourth story is that of the dormitories, airy rooms, with twelve beds in each. These rooms are arranged as below, along the two sides of a corridor, and divided in the same manner into the senior and junior side. A non-commissioned officer is lodged at each end of the corridor to see that order is kept.

Such is the building into which at the beginning of November the successful candidates from the *Lycées* and the *Ecoles préparatoires* are introduced, in age resembling the pupils whom the highest classes of English public schools send annually to the universities, and in number equal perhaps to the new under-graduates at one of the largest colleges at Cambridge. There is not, however, in other points much that is common, least of all in the methods and habits of study we are about to describe. This will be best understood by a summary of a day's work.

The students are summoned to rise at half-past five, have to answer the roll-call at six, from six to eight are to occupy themselves in study, and at eight they go to breakfast. On any morning except Wednesday, at half-past eight, we should find the whole of the new admission assembled in an amphitheater, permanent seats in which are assigned to them by lot, and thus placed they receive a lecture from a professor, rough notes of which they are expected to take while it goes on. The first half hour of the hour and a half assigned to each lecture is occupied with questions put by the professor relating to the previous lecture. A name is drawn by lot, the student on whom the lot falls is called up to the blackboard at which the professor stands, and is required to work a problem and answer questions. The lecture concluded, the pupils are conducted to the *salles d'étude*, which have just been described, where they are to study. Here for one hour they devote themselves to completing and writing out in full the notes of the lecture they have just heard. The professor and his assistants, the *répétiteurs*, are expected to follow and make a circuit through the corridors, to give an opportunity to ask for information on any difficult points in the lecture. A lithographed summary of the substance of the lecture, extending perhaps to two octavo pages, is also furnished to each studying room for the use of its pupils.

The lecture, as we have said, commences at half-past eight o'clock; it lasts an hour and a half; the hour of writing up the notes brings us to eleven. The young men are now relieved by a change of occupation, and employ themselves (still in their places in the rooms of study) at drawing. A certain number, detached from the rest, are sent to the physical and chemical laboratories. The rotation is such as to admit each student once a month to two or three hours' work at a furnace for chemistry, and once in two months to make experiments in electricity, or other similar subjects. In this way, either at their drawing or in the laboratories, they spend three hours, and at two o'clock go to their dinner in the refectories below, and after dinner are free to amuse themselves in the court-yard, the library, the fencing and the billiard rooms, till five. At five they return to the studying rooms, and for two hours, on Mondays and Fridays, they may employ themselves on any work they please (*étude libre;*) on Tuesday there is a lecture in French literature, and on Thursday in German; at seven o'clock they commence a lesson, which lasts till nine, in landscape and figure drawing, or they do exercises in French writing or in German ; at nine they go down to supper; at half-past nine they have to answer to a roll-call in their bedrooms, and at ten all the lights are put out.

Wednesday is a half-holiday, and the pupils are allowed to leave the school after two o'clock, and be absent till ten at night. The morning is occupied either in study, at the pleasure of the students, or in set exercises till eleven, when there is a lecture of one hour and a half, followed, as usual, by an hour of special study on the subject of the lecture. On Sunday they are allowed to be absent almost the whole day till ten P. M. There is no chapel, and apparently no common religious observance of any kind in the school.

Such is a general sketch of the ordinary employment of the day; a couple of hours of preparatory study before breakfast, a lecture on the differential calculus, on descriptive geometry, on chemistry, or natural philosophy, followed by an hour's work at notes; scientific drawing till dinner; recreation; and general study, or some lighter lecture in the evening. Were we merely to count the hours, we should find a result of eleven or eleven and a half hours of work for every day but Wednesday, and of seven and a half hours for that day. It is to be presumed, however, that though absolute idleness, sleeping, or reading any book not authorized for purposes of study, is strictly prohibited, and when detected, punished, nevertheless the strain on the attention during the hours of drawing and the lectures of the evening is by no means extreme. Landscape and figure drawing, the lecture in French literature, and probably that in German, may fairly be regarded as something like recreation. Such, at least, was the account given us of the lectures on literary subjects, and it agrees with the indifference to literature which marks the school. Of wholesome out-of-door recreation, there certainly seems to be a considerable want. There is nothing either of the English love of games, or of the skillful athletic gymnastics of the German schools.

The method of teaching is peculiar. The plan by which a vast number of students are collected as auditors of professorial lectures is one pursued in many academical institutions, at the Scotch universities, and in Germany. Large classes attend the lectures in Greek, in Latin, and in mathematics at Glasgow ; they listen to the professor's explanations, take notes, are occasionally questioned, and do all the harder work in their private lodgings. Such a system of course deserves in the fullest sense the epithet of voluntary ; a diligent student may make much of it; but there is nothing to compel an idle one to give any attention.

It seems to have been one especial object pursued in the Polytechnic to give to this plan of instruction, so lax in itself, the utmost possible stringency, and to accumulate upon it every attainable subsidiary appliance, every available safeguard against idleness. Questions are expressly put *vivâ voce* by the professor before his lecture; there is a subsequent hour of study devoted to the subject; there is the opportunity for explanation to individual students; the exaction of notes written out in full form; the professor also gives exercises to the students to write during their hours of general study, which he examines, and marks; general vivâ voce examinations (*interrogations générales*,) conducted by the professors and *répétiteurs*, follow the termination of each course of lectures; and lastly, one of the most important and peculiar parts of the method, we have what are called the *interrogations particulières*. After every five or six lectures in each subject, each student is called up for special questioning by one of the *répétiteurs*. The rooms in which these continual examinations are held have been described. They occupy one entire story of the building; each holds about six or eight pupils, with the *répétiteurs*. Every evening, except Wednesday, they are filled with these little classes, and busy with these close and personal questionings. A brief notice, at the utmost of twenty-four hours, is served upon the students who are thus to be called up. Generally, after they have had a certain number of lectures, they may expect that their time is at hand, but the precise hour of the summons can not be counted upon. The scheme is continually varied, and it defies, we are told, the efforts of the ablest young analysts to detect the law which it follows.

It will be seen at once that such a system, where, though nominally professorial, so little is left to the student's own voluntary action, where the ordinary study and *reading*, as it is called in our English universities (here such an expression is unknown) is subjected to such unceasing superintendence and surveillance, and to so much careful assistance, requires an immense staff of teachers. At the Polytechnic, for a maximum of 350 pupils, a body of fifteen professors and twenty-four *répétiteurs*, are employed, all solely in actual instruction, and in no way burdened with any part of the charge of the discipline or the finance, or even with the great yearly examinations for the passage from the first to the second division, and for the entrance to the public services.

With a provision of one instructor to every eight students, it is probable that in England we should avoid any system of large classes, from the fear of the inferior pupils being unable to keep pace with the more advanced. We should have numerous small classes, and should endeavor, above all things, to obtain the advantage of equality of attainment in the pupils composing them.

The French, on the other hand, make it their first object to secure one able principal teacher in each subject, a professor whom they burden with very few lectures. And to meet the educational difficulty thus created, to keep the whole large class of listeners up to the prescribed point, they call in this numerous and busily employed corps of assistants to *repeat*, to go over the professor's work afresh, to whip in, as it were, the stragglers and hurry up the loiterers. Certainly, one would think, a difficult task with a class of 170 freshmen in such work as the integral and differential calculus. It is one, however, in which they are aided by a stimulus which evidently acts most powerfully on the students of the Polytechnic School. During the two years of their stay, the prospect of their final admission to the public services can rarely be absent from the thoughts even of the least energetic and forethinking of the young men. Upon their place in the last class list will depend their fortune for life. A high position will secure them not only reputation, but the certainty of lucrative employment; will put it in their power to select which service they please, and in whichever they choose will secure them favorable notice. Let it be remembered that fifty-three of these one hundred and seventy are free scholars, born of parents too poor to pay 40*l.* a year for their instruction, to whom industry must be at all times a necessity, and industry during their two years at the Polytechnic the best conceivable expenditure, the most certainly remunerative investment of their pains and labor. The place on the final class list is obviously the prize for which this race of two years' length has to be run. What is it determines that place? Not by any means a final struggle before the winning-post, but steady effort and diligence from first to last throughout the course. For the order of the class list is not solely determined by success in the examination after which it is drawn up, but by the result of previous trials and previous work during the whole stay at the school.

For, during the whole time, every written exercise set by the professor, every drawing, the result of every *interrogation particulière* by the *répétiteurs*, and of each general interrogation by the professors and *répétiteurs*, is carefully marked, and a credit placed according to the name of the student and reserved for his benefit in the last general account. The marks obtained in the examination which closes the first year of study form a large element in this last calculation. It had been found that the work of the first year was often neglected: the evil was quickly remedied by this expedient. The student, it would seem, must feel that he is gaining or losing in his banking account, so to call it, by every day's work; every portion of his studies will tell directly for or against him in the final competition, upon which so much depends.

Such is the powerful mechanism by which the French nation forces out of the mass of boys attending their ordinary schools the talent and the science which they need for their civil and military services. The efforts made for admission to this great scientific school of the public services, the struggle for the first places at the exit from it, must be more than enough, it is thought, to establish the habits of hard work, to accumulate the information and attainment, and almost to create the ability which the nation requires for the general good.

We may now follow the student through his course of two years' study. The first year's work may be mainly divided into three portions of unequal length; two of them of about four months each (with an additional fortnight of private study and examination,) are mainly given to hard lecturing, whilst the third portion of two months is devoted to private study and to the examinations.

In accordance with this arrangement of the year, the four hardest subjects are thus distributed. Analysis and descriptive geometry, the staple work of the school—its Latin, as M. de Barante called it—come in the first four months; there is then a pause for private study and a general examination in these two subjects (*interrogations générales* as distinct from the *interrogations particulières* of the *répétiteurs.*) This brings us to the middle of March. Analysis and geometry are then laid aside for the rest of the year, and for the next portion of four months the pupils work at mechanics and geodesy, private study and a general examination completing this course also. Important lectures on physics and chemistry run on during both these periods, and are similarly closed by private study and a general examination. The less telling evening classes of French literature and German end at the beginning of June, and landscape and figure drawing only last half the year. It may be observed also, that, as a general rule, there is on each day one, and only one, really difficult lecture. This is immediately preceded and followed by private study, but then comes something lighter, as a relief, such as drawing or work in the laboratories.

The chief feature in the third portion of the year is the complete break in the lectures for general private study (*étude libre,*) a month or six weeks before the closing examination at the end of the year. The immediate prospect of this prevents any undue relaxing of the work; and it is curious to observe here how private efforts and enforced system are combined together, for even the private efforts are thus systematized and directed. The closing examination of the first year begins on the 1st and ends on the 25th of September.

The total number of lectures in each branch of study, with the dates when they respectively commence and finish, and the period when the general examinations (*interrogations générales*) take place, are exhibited in the following tables, and we should add that the interval between the close of each course and the commencement of the chief yearly examination is devoted to free study.

TABLE FOR THE SECOND OR LOWER DIVISION, FOLLOWING THE FIRST YEAR'S COURSE OF STUDY.

Subject of Study.	No. of Lectures.	Course of Lectures.		General Examinations. *Interrogations Générales.*		Annual Examination.
		Commenced.	Finished.	Commenced.	Finished.	
Analysis, ...	48	3rd Nov.	25th Feb.	13th March.	18th March.	Begins on the 1st Sept., and ends on the 25th Sept.
Mechanics and Machines, ...	40	21st March.	29th June.	24th July.	2nd August.	
Descriptive Geometry,	38	3rd Nov.	3rd March.	13th March.	18th March.	
Physics, ...	34	2nd "	28th June.	10th July.	19th July.	
Chemistry, ...	38	5th "	17th "	10th "	19th "	
Goedesy, ...	35	20th March	30th "	24th "	2nd August.	
French Literature, ...	30	8th Nov.	6th "			
German, ...	30	2nd "				
Figure and Landscape			15th "			
Drawing, ...	50	4th "	28th April.			
Total, ...	343					

The work of the second year is almost identical in its general plan with that of the first. A continuation of analysis with mechanics in place of descriptive geometry is the work of the first four months, then comes the private study and the *interrogations générales*, and then again, from the middle of March to the middle of July, work of a more professional character, stereotomy, the art of war and topography, forms the natural completion of the pupil's studies. Chemistry and physics follow the same course as during the first year, and terminate with the private study and the general examination at the beginning of August. The evening lectures in French literature and German end about the middle of June, and those in figure and landscape drawing at the beginning of May. The last portion is again given to private study and the great Final Examination.

TABLE FOR THE FIRST OR UPPER DIVISION, FOLLOWING THE SECOND YEAR'S COURSE OF STUDY.

Subject of Study.	No. of Lectures.	Course of Lectures.		General Examinations. *Interrogations Générales.*		Annual Examination.
		Commenced,	Finished.	Commenced.	Finished.	
Analysis, ...	32	11th Nov.	3rd March.	13th March.	18th March.	Begins on the 10th Sept. and ends on the 10th Oct.
Mechanics and Machines, ...	42	10th "	2nd "	13th "	18th "	
Stereotomy, ...	32	20th March.	26th June.	10th July.	19th July.	
Physics, ...	36	12 Nov.	29th "	24th "	2nd Aug.	
Chemistry, ...	38	14th "	28th "	24th July.	2nd "	
Architecture and Construction, ...	40	10th "	8th "	....	....	
Military Art and Fortification, ...	20	21st March.	21st "	10th "	19th July.	
Topography, ...	10	3rd Jan.				
French Literature, ...	30	11th Nov.	9th "			
German, ...	30	14th "	19th "			
Figure and Landscape Drawing, ...	48	12th "	2nd May.			
Total, ...	358					

V. THE EXAMINATIONS, PARTICULARLY THAT OF THE FIRST YEAR AND THE FINAL ONE.

We have now brought the pupil nearly to the end of his career, but must previously say a few words about his examinations, the chief epochs which mark his progress, and the last of which fixes his position almost for life. For this purpose it is necessary to recapitulate briefly what has been said in different places of the whole examinatorial system of the Polytechnic School.

1. All the professors require the students in their studying rooms, to answer questions in writing on the courses as they go through them: a different question is given to each student, and every third question is of such a nature as to involve a numerical example in the reply.

These questions are given in the proportion of one to about every four lectures, and the replies after being examined by the professor or *répétiteur*, are indorsed with a credit, varying from 0 to 20, and the paper is then given back to the student, to be produced at the close of the year.

2. Credits are assigned to the students for their ordinary manipulations in chemistry and physics, during the first year; and at the close of each year, for their manipulations, in chemistry alone, before the examiners.

3. The *répétiteurs* examine, (in the *interrogations particulières,*) every ten or fourteen days, from six to eight students during a sitting of two hours, on the subject of study lectured on since the previous examination of the same kind. All these students must continue present, and at the close the *répétiteur* assigns to each a

previous examination of the same kind. All these students must continue present, and at the close the *répétiteur* assigns to each a credit entirely dependent on the manner in which each has replied. The professors and captains inspectors are occasionally present at these examinations, which are discontinued at certain periods according to the instructions of the director of studies.

4. At different intervals of time, from a fortnight to a month, as may happen, after the close of the course in each branch of study, general examinations (*interrogations générales*) are made by the professors and *répétiteurs.* From four to six students are examined together for at least two hours, and at the conclusion the professor makes known to the director of studies the credit he has granted to each student for the manner in which he has passed his examination.

Such may be called the minor or ordinary examinations. But there is an annual closing examination at the end of each year, which we will now describe. The first year's annual examination commences on the 1st and ends on the 25th September. It is carried on by special examiners, (a different set from those who conduct the entrance examinations,) and not by the professors. These give to every student a credit between 0 and 20 in each branch of study, according to the manner in which he replies.

The following table shows the co-efficients of influence allowed to the different studies of the first year, subdivided also among the particular classes of examination to which the student has been subjected. The component parts of the co-efficients as well as the co-efficients themselves, slightly vary from year to year, dependent on the number of examinations :—

TABLE I.—FIRST YEAR'S COURSE OF STUDIES: SECOND DIVISION.

Nature of Study.	Total Co-efficients.	Co-efficient of Influence awarded to								
		Written Answers to Professors' Questions.	Examinations by *Répétiteurs.* (*Int. Part.*)	General Examinations. (*Int. Gén.*)	Manipulations. Ordinary.	Manipulations. At Examinations.	Sheets of notes on descriptive Geometry.	Graphical Representations and Drawing.	First Annual Examination.	Total Co-efficients.
Analysis, ...	56	9	10	9	..	..	..	..	28	56
Mechanics, ...	60	7	9	8	..	..	..	14	22	60
Descriptive Geometry, ...	48	..	7	7	..	..	4	12	18	48
Geodesy, ...	39	6	5	7	..	..	..	3	18	39
Physics, ...	45	6	9	7	2	..	..	..	21	45
Chemistry, ...	45	5	9	7	4	2	..	..	18	45
French Literature, ...	12	12	..	..	..	..	..	..	..	12
German Language, ...	10	2	3	..	..	..	..	..	5	10
Drawing, ...	10	..	..	..	..	..	..	10	..	10
Shading and Tinting Plans,	3	..	..	..	..	..	..	3	..	3

At the conclusion of this examination the director of studies pre pares a statement for each student, exhibiting the credits he has obtained at each of the preceding examinations in each subject, multiplied by the co-efficient of influence, and the sum of the products represents the numerical account of the student's credit in each branch of study.

As the process is somewhat intricate, we append the following example, to show the nature of the calculation performed, in order to ascertain the amount of credits due to each student:—

REPORT OF THE CREDITS GAINED IN THE FIRST YEAR'S COURSE OF STUDY BY M. N., STUDENT AT THE POLYTECHNIC SCHOOL.

Subject of Examination.	Co-efficient of Influence.	Nature of Examination or Proof.	Credit obtained by the Student.	Co-efficients of Influence.	Product.	Sum of Products.	Mean Credit in each Subject of the Course.
Analysis,.........	56	Written answers to Professors' questions,.................	17.16	9	154.44	845.81	15.09
		Examinations by *répétiteurs* (*interrogations particulières*,)	15.47	10	154.70		
		General Examination (*interrogations générales*,)......	13.71	9	123.39		
		Annual Examination,........	14.75	28	413.28		
Mechanics,.......	60	Written answers to Professors' questions, ...	13.45	7	94.15	664.13	11.07
		Examinations by *répétiteurs*,	12.72	9	114.48		
		General examination,........	11.37	8	90.96		
		Graphical representations and drawing, ...	5.61	14	78.54		
		Annual examination,........	13.00	22	286.00		
Descriptive Geometry, ...	48	Examinations by *répétiteurs*,	17.15	7	120.05	633.15	13.19
		General examination,........	11.72	7	82.04		
		Sheets of notes,.............	12.45	4	49.80		
		Graphical rep. and drawing,..	11.88	12	142.76		
		Annual examination,........	13.25	18	238.50		
Geodesy, ...	39	Written answers to Professors' questions,.................	9 16	6	54.96	229.01	5.87
		Examinations by *répétiteurs*,	7.85	5	39.25		
		General examination,......	5.74	7	40.18		
		Graphical rep. and drawing,..	4.36	3	13.08		
		Annual examination,........	4.53	1	81.54		
Physics,..........	45	Written answers to Professors' questions, ...	2.76	6	16.56	112.21	2.49
		Examinations by *répétiteurs*,	3.54	9	31.86		
		General examination,......	3.15	7	22.05		
		Ordinary manipulation,......	1.55	2	3.10		
		Annual examination,........	1.84	21	38.84		
Chemistry, ...	45	Written answers to Professors' questions, ...	2.46	5	12.30	131.16	2.91
		Examinations by *repétiteurs*,	3.25	9	29.95		
		General examination,........	2.47	7	17,29		
		Ordinary manipulation.......	2.26	4	9 04		
		Manipulation at examination,	1.58	2	3.16		
		Annual examination,........	3.34	18	60.12		
French Literature,	12	Written answers to Professors' questions, ...	5.64	12	67.68	67.68	5.64
German Language,	10	Written answers to Professors' questions,................	6.57	2	13.14	55.92	5.59
		Examinations by *répétiteurs*,	4.86	3	14.58		
		Annual examination,.......	5.64	5	28.20		
Drawing, ...	10	Graphical representations and drawing, ...	4,36	10	43.60	43.60	4.36
Shading and Tinting Plans,	3	Graphical representations and drawing, ...	3.86	3	11.58	11.58	3.86

Sum,............10)70.07

General Mean Credit, = (7.00)

It is important to remark that any student whose *mean credit*, given in the eighth column of the preceding table, in any branch of study does not exceed *three*, or whose *general mean credit* for the whole of the studies being the arithmetical mean of all the values recorded in the eighth column, and given at the bottom in the example, does not exceed six, is *considered to possess an insufficient amount of instruction to warrant his being permitted to pass into the first division for the second year's course.* He is accordingly excluded from the school, unless he has been prevented from pursuing his studies by illness, in which case, when the facts are thoroughly established, he will be allowed a second year's study in the second division, comprising the first year's course of study.

We now pass to the second annual or great final examination for admission to the public services, remarking only that in the *interrogations générales* of the second year the principal subjects of both years are included.

The final examinations for admission into the public service commence about the 10th September, and last about one month. They are conducted by the same examiners who examined at the close of the first year. These are five in number, and appointed by the minister of war. One of these takes analysis; a second, mechanics; a third, descriptive geometry and geodesy; the fourth, physics; and the fifth, chemistry.

The examination in military art and topography is conducted by a captain of engineers specially appointed for the purpose; and in the same manner the examination in German is carried on by a professor, usually a civilian, specially but not permanently appointed.

The questions are oral, and extend over the whole course of study pursued during the two years. Each student is taken separately for one hour and a quarter on different days by each of the five examiners; each examiner examines about eight students daily.

A table, very similar to that already given, is prepared under the superintendence of the Director of studies for every student, to ascertain the numerical amount of his credits in each branch of study, the co-efficients of influences for the particular subject of study and nature of examination being extracted from a table similar to that in page 80, and when these tables have all been completed, a general list of all the students is made out, arranged in the order of their merits.

Formerly, conduct was permitted to exercise some slight influence on their position, but that is no longer the case.

The same regulations exist, as regards the minimum amount of credit that will entitle the students to enter into the public service, as have already been stated above in reference to the passage from the first to the second year's course of study.

TABLE II. SECOND YEAR'S COURSE OF STUDY: FIRST DIVISION.

	Total Co-efficients.	Co-efficient of Influence awarded to										
		Result of previous Year's Examination.	Written answers to Professors' Questions.	Examinations by *Répétiteurs. (Int. Part.)*	General Examinations. *(Int. Gén.)*	Manipulation. Ordinary.	Manipulation. At Examinations.	Sketches and Notes in Architecture.	Graphical Representations and Drawing.	Examination in Architecture.	Second Annual or Final Examination.	Total Co-efficients.
Analysis,	81	28	8	10	9						26	81
Mechanics,	92	25	8	12	9				10		28	92
Descriptive Geometry,	36	36										36
Geodesy,	37		6	5	7				1		18	37
Physics,	68	23	5	10	8						22	68
Chemistry,	68	20	5	10	8	4	2				19	68
Architecture,	36							12	14	10		36
Military art and Topography,	25			3	5				9		8	25
French Literature,	18	6	12									18
German,	15	5	2	3								15
Drawing,	15	5							10			15
Shading and Tinting,	5	2							3			5

From the preceding tables and explanations, it will be apparent that, as the whole of the students for each year are compelled to follow precisely the same course of study, the system of professorial instruction, combined with the constant tutelage and supervision exercised by the *répétiteurs*, and the examinations (*interrogations particulières*) of the *répétiteurs*, at short intervals of time, have for their principal object the keeping alive in the minds of the students the information which has been communicated to them. As a stimulus to continuous and unceasing exertion, it will be seen by an inspection of the tables of the co-efficients of influence, that the manner in which the students acquit themselves from day to day, and from week to week, is made an element, and a very important one, in determining their final position in the list arranged according to merit, exceeding as it does in most instances the influence exerted on their classification by their final examination at the close of each year. This principle thus recognizes not only their knowledge at the end of each year, but also the manner in which they have proved it to the professors and *répétiteurs* in the course of the year; and with reference to the second year's study, the final result of the first year's classification exercises an influence amounting to about one-third of the whole, in the final classification at the end of the second year.

It follows also, that as the examinations at the end of each year are made by examiners, otherwise unconnected with the school, and not by the professors belonging to it, the positions of the students in the classified list is partly dependent on the judgment of the professors with whom they are constantly in communication, and partly on the public examiners, whom they meet only in the examination rooms.*

The examiners of the students are not frequently changed, and practically the same may be said of the examiners for admission.

The students at the head of the list have generally since the wars of the first Empire entered into the civil rather than into the military services, the former being much better remunerated.

The services are usually selected by preference, nearly in the following order:—

The Roads and Bridges (*Ponts et chaussées*) and Mines (*Mines,*) - - - - } very nearly on an equality.
Powder and Saltpetre (*Poudres et Salpêtres.*)
Naval Architects (*Génie maritime.*)
Engineers (*Génie militaire.*)
The Artillery (*Artillerie de terre,*) and the Staff Corps (*Etat Major,*) } very nearly on an equality.
The Hydographical Corps (*Ingénieurs Hydrographes.*)

Subjects of Study.	Per-centage of influence exercised on the position of the Students.						
	During the 1st Year.		During the 2nd Year.			In the Classified List at the end of 2nd year.	
	By Professors and *Répétiteurs.*	By Examiners.	By the results of the first Year's Examination.	By Professors and *Répétiteurs.*	By Examiners.	By Professors and *Répétiteurs.*	By Examiners.
Analysis,	50.0	50.0	34.5	32.5	33.0	49.75	50.25
Mechanics,	63.2	36.7	27.2	42.4	30.4	59.6	40.40
Descriptive Geometry,	62.5	37.5	100.0	0.0	0.0	62.5	37.5
Geodesy,	53.8	46.2	0.0	51.4	48.6	*51.4	48.6
Physics,	53.3	46.7	33.8	33.8	32.4	51.8	48.2
Chemistry,	60.0	40.0	29.4	43.2	27.4	60.8	39.2
Architecture,	......	......	0.0	100.0	0.0	100.0	100.0
Military Art and Topography,	......	......	0.0	68.0	32.0	68.0	32.0
French Literature,	100.0	0.0	33.3	66.7	0.0	100.0	0.0
German Language,	100.0	0.0	33.3	33.3	33.4	66.7	33.3
Drawing,	100.0	0.0	33.3	66.7	0.0	100.0	0.0
Shading and Tinting Plans,	100.0	0.0	40.0	60.0	0.0	100.0	0.0
					*	* When taught in the 2nd year.	

* The influence exercised in the various branches of study, and consequently in the position of the students in the list classified according to merit, by the professors and *répétiteurs* on the one hand, and by the examiners on the other, as in the table above.

Tobacco Department (*Administration des Tabacs.*)
Telegraph Department (*Lignes Télégraphiques.*)
Navy (*Marine.*)
Marine Artillery (*Artillerie de mer.*)

Such, at least, is the result of a comparison of the selections made by the students during eight different years.

This preference of the civil to the military services has been the subject of frequent complaints on the part of the military authorities to the minister of war.

No steps have, however, been taken by the French government to prevent the *free* choice of a profession being granted to the most successful students.

We have now followed the student at the Polytechnic to the end of his school career. He is then to pass to his particular School of Application, in which (as the name implies) he is taught to apply his science to practice. It is difficult to state precisely the amount of such science which the highest pupils may be thought to possess on leaving; the best idea of it will be gained by reference to the programmes of the most important of the lectures. It is also needless to dwell again on the main features of the school—the emulation called forth, the minute method, the great prizes offered for sustained labor. We must, however, make some remarks on these points before concluding our account, so far as they bear on the subject of military education.

VI. GENERAL REMARKS.

1. Keeping out of sight for the moment some defects both in the principles and details of the education of this school, the method of teaching adopted seems to us excellent, and worthy of careful study. In this remark we allude principally to the skillful combination of two methods which have been generally thought incompatible; for it unites the well-prepared lecture of a German professor, with the close personal questioning of a first-rate English school or college lecture. But besides this, its whole system is admirably adapted for the class of pupils it educates.

These pupils are generally not of the wealthy classes; they are able, and struggling for a position in life. On all these grounds their own assistance in the work may be calculated upon. Yet they are not left to themselves to make the most of their professors' lectures. The aid of *répétiteurs*, even more valuable in its constant "prudent interrogations," than in the explanations afforded, is joined to the stimulus given by marking every step of proficiency, and by making all tell on the last general account. But though the routine and method of the school are so elaborate, play is given to the individual freedom of the pupils in their private work, and this is managed so skillfully that the private work is made immediately to precede the final examination, on which mainly depends the pupil's place for life. Thus from first to last they are carried on by their system without being cramped by it; every circumstance favorable to study is made the most of; rigorous habit, mental readiness, the power of working with others, and the power of working for themselves, the ambition for immediate and permanent success, all the objects and all the methods which students ever have in view, support and stimulate those of the Polytechnic in their two years' career.

2. The mainspring, however, of the school's energy is the competition amongst the pupils themselves, and this could hardly exist without the great prizes offered to the successful. This advantage, added to the general impulse of the early days of the Empire, has no doubt powerfully contributed to the great position of the school. It has made it a kind of university of the *élite* mathematicians, and as in England young men look to the prizes of the universities, and the professions to which they lead, as their best opening in life, so in France, ever since the first revolution, the corresponding class has inclined to the active and chiefly military career which is offered by the great competitive school of the country.

3. A preparatory school of this remarkable character can not but exercise a very powerful influence over those three-fourths of its pupils who leave it to enter the army. The obvious question is whether the attempt is not made to teach more than is either necessary or desirable for military purposes, and to this suspicion may be added the fact that the civil prizes being more in request than the military, many of those who enter the army do so in the first instance reluctantly, and that the pupils at the bottom of the list appear to be often such marked failures as to imply either great superficiality or premature exhaustion.

4. In studying the Polytechnic School we have had these points constantly brought before us, and feeling the difficulty of discussing them fully, we beg to invite attention to the evidence sent us in reply to some questions which we addressed on the subject to some distinguished scientific officers and civilians connected with the school. We will give briefly the result of our own inquiries.

5. The complaint of General Paixhans has been quoted. He urges that a considerable proportion of the army pupils are mere *queues de promotion*, and quite insufficient to form *le corps et surtout la tête* of troops *d'élite.*

Other not inconsistent complaints we heard ourselves, of the mental exhaustion and the excessively abstract tendencies of many of the military pupils of the school.

6. Such are the complaints. There is certainly reason to think that, with regard to the twenty or thirty lowest pupils on the list, those of General Paixhans are well founded. These are the *breaks down*, and we are at first surprised that, entering as they must do,* with high attain-

* The students are selected, by a competitive examination, out of a very large number of candidates, as will be seen from the following table, extracted from the yearly calendars :—

Year.	Candidates who inscribed their Names.	Candidates examined.	Candidates admitted to the Polytechnic.	Year.	Candidates who inscribed their Names.	Candidates examined.	Candidates admitted to the Polytechnic.
1832	567	468	183	1839	530	531	135
1833	367	304	110	.....	....	....	....
1834	627	541	150	1842	709	559	137
1835	729	633	154	1843	802	559	166
.....	....	....	....	1844	746	531	143
1837	629	508	137	1845	780	559	136
1838	533	410	131				

Giving an average of one student for four candidates *examined*, so that it is impossible to imagine that there is any lack of ability in those selected.

A similar result appears to follow from some other more recent statistics.

ments, they should fall so low as the marks in the tables (with which we are most liberally supplied) prove to be the case.

At the same time, we believe that no teaching ever has provided or will provide against many failures out of one hundred and seventy pupils, even among those who promised well at first: and if the standard of the majority of pupils is high at the Polytechnique, and the point reached by the first few *very* high, it is no reproach that the descent amongst the last few should be very rapid.

With regard to the assertion, that the teaching is excessive and leads too much to abstract pursuits for soldiers, it may be partially true. Perhaps the general passion for science has led to an overstrained teaching for the army, even for its scientific corps; and yet would it be allowed by officers of the highest scientific ability, either in the French or the English army, that less science is required for the greatest emergencies of military than for those of civil engineering, or for the theory of projectiles than for working the department of saltpetre?

It may, however, be true that an attempt is made at the Polytechnic to exact *from all* attainments which can only be reached by *a few*.

7. With this deduction, we must express our opinion strongly in favor of the influence of the Polytechnic on the French army. We admit that in some instances pupils who have failed in their attempt at civil prizes enter the army unwillingly, but they are generally soon penetrated with its *esprit de corps*, and they carry into it talent which it would not otherwise have obtained. Cases of overwork no doubt occur, as in the early training for every profession, but (following the evidence we have received) we have no reason to think them so numerous as to balance the advantage of vigorous, thoughtful study directed early towards a profession which, however practical, is eminently benefited by it. "It can not be said," was the verdict of one well fitted to express an opinion, "that there is too much science in the French army."

8. Assuming, however, the value of the scientific results produced in the French army by the Polytechnic, it by no means follows that a similar institution would be desirable in another country. Without much discussion it may be safely said that the whole history and nature of the institution—the offspring of a national passion for system and of revolutionary excitement—make it thoroughly peculiar to France.

9. Some obvious defects must be noticed. The curious rule of forbidding the use of *all* books whatever is a very exaggerated attempt to make the pupil to rely entirely on the professors and *répétiteurs*. The exclusive practice of *oral* examination also seems to us a defect. Certainly every examination should give a pupil an opportunity of showing such

Year.	Number of Candidates who inscribed their Names.	Number declared admissible to the Second Examination.	Number admitted.
1852	510	216	202
1853	494	222	217
1854	519	238	170
1855	544	232	170

In judging, however, of these numbers, it should be borne in mind that a very large number of the candidates who succeed have tried more than once; the successful of this year have been among the unsuccessful of last year, so that the proportion of individuals who succeed to individuals who fail, is, of course, considerably larger than one to four. Of the 170 candidates admitted in November, 1855, 117 had put down their names for the examination of 1854, and 53 only had not been previously inscribed. Of the 117 who put down their names, 19 had withdrawn without being examined at all, 71 had been rejected on the preliminary examination, 27 had been unsuccessful at that of the second degree; 98 of the 170 came up for the second time to the examination.

valuable qualities as readiness and power of expression; but an examination solely oral appears to us an uncertain test of depth or accuracy of knowledge; and however impartial or practiced an examiner may be, it is impossible that questions put orally can present exactly the same amount of difficulty, and so be equally fair, to the several competitors.

At the same time, although in all great competing examinations the chief part of the work (in our opinion) should be *written*, the constant oral cross-questioning of the minor examinations at the Polytechnic, appeared to be one of the most stimulating and effective parts of their system.

10. A more serious objection than any we have named lies against the exclusive use of mathematical and scientific training, to the neglect of all other, as almost the only instrument of education. The spirit of the school, as shown especially by its entrance examinations, is opposed to any literary study. This is a peculiar evil in forming characters for a liberal profession like the army. Such a plan may indeed produce striking results, if the sole object is to create distinguished mathematicians, though even then the acuteness in one direction is often accompanied by an unbalanced and extravagant judgment in another. But a great school should form the whole and not merely a part of the man; and as doing this, as strengthening the whole mind, instead of forcing on one or two of its faculties—as giving, in a word, what is justly called a *liberal* education—we are persuaded that the system of cultivating the taste for historical and other similar studies, as well as for mere science, is based on a sounder principle than that which has produced the brilliant results of the Polytechnic.

11. It may be added, in connection with the above remark, that as the entrance examination at the Polytechnic influences extensively the teaching of the great French schools, and is itself almost solely mathematical, it tends to diffuse a narrow and exclusive pursuit of science, which is very alien from the spirit of English teaching.

12. We may sum up our remarks on the Polytechnic School thus:—

Regarded simply as a great Mathematical and Scientific School, its results in producing eminent men of science have been extraordinary. It has been the great (and a truly great) Mathematical University of France.

Regarded again as a Preparatory School for the public works, it has given a very high scientific education to civil engineers, whose scientific education in other countries (and amongst ourselves) is believed to be much slighter and more accidental.

Regarded as a school for the scientific corps of the army, its peculiar mode of uniting in one course of competition candidates for civil and military services, has probably raised scientific thought to a higher point in the French than in any other army.

Regarded as a system of teaching, the method it pursues in developing the talents of its pupils appears to us the best we have ever studied.

It is in its studies and some of its main principles that the example of the Polytechnic School may be of most value. In forming or improving any military school, we can not shut our eyes to the successful working at the Polytechnic of the principle, which it was the first of all schools to initiate, the making great public prizes the reward and stimulus of the pupil's exertions. We may observe how the state has here encouraged talent by bestowing so largely assistance upon all successful, but poor pupils, during their school career. We may derive some lessons from its method of teaching, though the attempt to imitate it might be unwise. Meanwhile, without emulating the long established scientific prestige of the Polytechnic, we have probably amongst ourselves abundant materials for a military scientific education, at least as sound as that given at this great School.

NOTE.

In addition to the Schools of Application for Artillery and Engineers at Metz, and of Infantry and Cavalry at St. Cyr, of which a pretty full account will be given, the following Public Services are supplied by the Polytechnic School.

Gunpowder and Saltpetre.—(*Poudres et Salpêtres.*)

In France the manufacture of gunpowder is solely in the hands of the Government. The pupils of the Polytechnic who enter the gunpowder and saltpetre service, are sent in succession to different powder-mills and saltpetre refineries, so as to gain a thorough acquaintance with all the details of the manufacture.

On first entering the service they are named *élèves des poudres*. They afterwards rise successively to the rank of assistant-commissary, commissary of the third, of the second, and of the first class.

Navy.—(*Marine.*)

A small number of the pupils of the Polytechnic enter the Navy. They receive the rank of *élève de première classe*, from the date of their admission.

They are sent to the ports to serve afloat. After two years' service they may be promoted to the rank of *enseigne de vaisseau*, on passing the necessary examinations, on the same terms precisely as the *élèves de première classe* of the Naval School.

Marine Artillery.—(*Artillerie de la Marine.*)

The French marine artillery differs from the English corps of the same name, in not serving afloat. Its duties are confined to the ports and to the colonies. It is governed by the same rules and ordinances as the artillery of the army.

The foundries of La Villeneuve, Rochefort, Ruelle, Névers, and Saint Gervais are under its direction.

The officers of the marine artillery are liable to be sent on board ship to study naval gunnery, so as to be in a position to report upon alterations or improvements in this science.

Naval Architects.—(*Génie Maritime.*)

The naval architects are charged with the construction and repair of vessels of war, and with the manufacture of all the machinery required in the ports and dockyards. The factories of Indret and La Chaussade are under their direction.

The pupils of the Polytechnic enter the corps of naval architects with the rank of *élève du Génie Maritime.* They are sent to the School of Application of Naval Architects at L'Orient. After two years' instruction they undergo an examination, and, if successful, they are promoted to the rank of sub-architect of the third class, so far as vacancies admit. They may be advanced to the second class after a service of two years.

Hydrographers.—(*Ingénieurs Hydrographes.*)

The hydrographers are stationed at Paris. They are sent to the coast to make surveys, and the time so spent reckons as a campaign in determining their pension. On their return to Paris they are employed in the construction of maps and charts.

The hydrographers have the same rank and advantage as the naval architects.

On leaving the Polytechnic, the pupils enter the corps of hydrographers with the rank of *élève hydrographe.* After two years' service, and one season employed on the coast, they become sub-hydrographers without further examination.

ROADS AND BRIDGES.—GOVERNMENT CIVIL ENGINEERS.—(*Ponts et Chaussées.*)

The Polytechnic furnishes exclusively the pupils for the Government Civil Engineer Corps. On leaving the Polytechnic, the pupils enter the School of Application in Paris. The course of instruction here extends over a period of three years. It commences each year on the first of November, and lasts till the 1st of April. After the final examination, the pupils are arranged according to the results of the examination and the amount of work performed.

The pupils enter the college with the rank of *élève de troisième classe.* They rise successively to the second and to the first class, on making the requisite progress in their studies.

From the 1st of May to the 1st of November the *élèves* of the second and the third class are sent on duty into the provinces. The *élèves* of the first class who have completed their three years' course of instruction, are employed in the duties of ordinary engineers, or are detached on special missions. In about three years after quitting the college, they may be appointed ordinary engineers of the second class.

The engineers of the *Ponts et Chaussées* prepare the projects and plans, and direct the execution of the works for the construction, preservation, and repair of high roads, and of the bridges and other structures connected with these roads, with navigable rivers, canals, seaports, lighthouses, &c. They are charged with the superintendence of railways, of works for draining marshes, and operations affecting water-courses; they report upon applications to erect factories driven by water. Under certain circumstances, they share with the Mining Engineers the duty of inspecting steam-engines.

Permission is not unfrequently granted to the engineers of the *Ponts et Chaussées* to accept private employment. They receive leave of absence for a certain time, retaining their rank and place in their corps, but without pay.

MINING ENGINEERS.—(*Mines.*)

The Mining School of Application is organized almost exactly on the same plan as that of the *Ponts et Chaussées:* like the latter, it is in Paris.

The course of instruction, which lasts three years, consists of lectures, drawing, chemical manipulation and analysis, visits to manufactories, geological excursions, and the preparation of projects for mines and machines. Journeys are made by the pupils, during the second half of the last two years of the course, into the mineral districts of France or foreign countries for the purpose of studying the practical details of mining. These journeys last one hundred days at least. The pupils are required to examine carefully the railroads and the geological features of the countries they pass through, and to keep a journal of facts and observations. In the final examination, marks are given for every part of their work.

The mining engineers, when stationed in the departments, are charged to see that the laws and ordinances relating to mines, quarries, and factories are properly observed, and to encourage, either directly or by their advice, the extension of all branches of industry connected with the extraction and treatment of minerals.

One of their principal duties is the superintendence of mines and quarries, in the three-fold regard of safety of the workmen, preservation of the soil, and economical extraction of the minerals.

They exercise a special control over all machines designed for the production of steam, and over railways, as far as regards the metal and fuel.

The instructors in the School of Application in Paris, and in the School of Mines at St. Etienne, are exclusively taken from the members of the corps.

Like the engineers of the *Ponts et Chaussées*, the mining engineers obtain permission to undertake private employment.

TOBACCO DEPARTMENT.—(*Administration des Tabacs.*)

The pupils who enter the tobacco service, commence, on quitting the Polytechnic, with the rank of *élève de 2e classe.* They study, in the manufactory at

Paris, chemistry, physics, and mechanics, as applied to the preparation of tobacco. They make themselves acquainted at the same time with the details of the manufacture and with the accounts and correspondence.

They are generally promoted to the rank of *élève de* 1re *classe* in two years. They rise afterwards successively to the rank of sub-inspector, inspector, and director.

After completing their instruction at the manufactory of Paris, the *élèves* are sent to tobacco manufactories in other parts of France.

Promotion in the tobacco service does not follow altogether by seniority. Knowledge of the manufacture and attention to their duties are much considered, as the interests of the treasury are involved in the good management of the service.

TELEGRAPHS.—(*Lignes Télégraphiques.*)

On entering the telegraphic service the pupils of the Polytechnic receive the rank of *élève inspecteur.*

They pass the first year at the central office. During the six winter months they study, under two professors, the composition of signals, and the regulations which insure their correctness and dispatch, the working of telegraphs and the manner of repairing them, the theory of the mode of tracing lines and of determining the height of the towers, electro-magnetism and its application to the electic telegraph. During the summer months they make tours of inspection. They assist in the execution of works, and practice leveling and the laying down of lines.

At the end of the year the *élèves inspecteurs* undergo an examination, and, if there are vacancies, are appointed provisional inspectors. After a year in this rank they may be appointed inspectors either in France or Algeria.

Each inspector has charge of a district containing from twelve to fifteen stations. He is obliged to make a tour of inspection once a month of at least ten days' duration.

After a certain number of years' service the inspector rises to the rank of director. Besides their other duties, the directors exercise a general superintendence over the inspectors.

PROGRAMMES OF THE PRINCIPAL COURSES OF INSTRUCTION

OF THE IMPERIAL POLYTECHNIC SCHOOL DURING THE TWO YEARS OF STUDY.

I. ANALYSIS.—*FIRST YEAR.*

DIFFERENTIAL CALCULUS.

LESSONS 1—9. *Derivatives and Differentials of Functions of a Single Variable.*

INDICATION of the original problems which led geometers to the discovery of the infinitesimal calculus.

Use of infinitesimals; condition, subject to which, two infinitely small quantities may be substituted for one another. Indication in simple cases of the advantage of such substitution.

On the different orders of infinitely small quantities. Infinitely small quantities of a certain order may be neglected in respect of those of an inferior order. The infinitely small increment of a function is in general of the same order as the corresponding increment of the variable, that is to say, their ratio has a finite limit.

Definitions of the derivative and differential of a function of a single variable. Tangents and normals to plane curves, whose equation in linear or polar co-ordinates is given.

A function is increasing or decreasing, according as its derivative is positive or negative. If the derivative is zero for all values of the variable, the function is constant. Concavity and convexity of curves; points of inflection.

Principle of function of functions. Differentiation of inverse functions.

Differentials of the sums, products, quotients, and powers of functions, whose differentials are known. General theorem for the differentiation of functions composed of several functions.

Differentials of exponential and logarithmic functions.

Differentials of direct and inverse circular functions.

Differentiation of implicit functions.

Tangents to curves of double curvature. Normal plane.

Differential of the area and arc of a plane curve, in terms of rectilinear and polar co-ordinates.

Differential of the arc of a curve of double curvature.

Applications to the cycloid, the spiral of Archimedes, the logarithmic spiral, the curve whose normal, sub-normal, or tangent, is constant; the curve whose normal passes through a fixed point; the curve whose arc is proportional to the angle which it subtends at a given point.

Derivatives and differentials of different orders of functions of one variable. Notation adopted.

Remarks upon the singular points of plane curves.

LESSONS—10—13. *Derivatives and Differentials of Functions of Several Variables.*

Partial derivatives and differentials of functions of several variables. The order in which two or any number of differentiations is effected does not influence the result.

Total differentials. Symbolical formula for representing the total differential of the nth order of a function of several independent variables.

Total differentials of different orders of a function; several dependent variables. Case where these variables are linear functions of the independent variables.

The infinitesimal increment of a function of several variables may in general be regarded as a linear function of the increments assigned to the variables. Exceptional cases.

Tangent and normal planes to curved surfaces.

LESSONS 14—18. *Analytical Applications of the Differential Calculus.*

Development of F $(x + h,)$ according to ascending powers of h. Limits within which the remainder is confined on stopping at any assigned power of h.

Development of F $(x,)$ according to powers of x or $x—a$; a being a quantity arbitrarily assumed. Application to the functions sin $(x,)$ cos x, a^x, $(1 + x^m)$ and log. $(1 + x.)$ Numerical applications. Representation of cos x and sin x by imaginary exponential quantities.

Developments of $\cos^m x$ and $\sin^m x$ in terms of sines and curves of multiples of x.

Development of F $(x + h, y + k,)$ according to powers of h and k. Development of F (x, y) according to powers of x and y. Expression for the remainder. Theorem on homogeneous functions.

Maxima and minima of functions of a single variable; of functions of several variables, whether independent or connected by given equations. How to discriminate between maxima and minima values in the case of one and two independent variables.

True values of functions, which upon a particular supposition assume one or another of the forms

$$\frac{0}{0}, \frac{\infty}{\infty}, \quad \infty + 0, \ 0^0, \ 4^\infty$$

LESSONS 19—23. *Geometrical Applications. Curvature of Plane Curves.*

Definition of the curvature of a plane curve at any point. Circle of curvature. Center of curvature. This center is the point where two infinitely near normals meet.

Radius of curvature with rectilinear and polar co-ordinates. Change of the independent variable.

Contacts of different orders of plane curves. Osculating curves of a given kind. Osculating straight line. Osculating circle. It is identical with the circle of curvature.

Application of the method of infinitesimals to the determination of the radius of curvature of certain curves geometrically defined. Ellipse, cycloid, epicycloid, &c.

Evolutes of plane curves. Value of the arc of the evolute. Equation to the involute of a curve. Application to the circle. Evolutes considered as envelops. On envelops in general. Application to caustics.

LESSONS 14—17. *Geometrical Applications continued. Curvature of Lines of Double Curvature and of Surfaces.*

Osculating plane of a curve of double curvature. It may be considered as passing through three points infinitely near to one another, or as drawn through a tangent parallel to the tangent infinitely near to the former. Center and radius of curvature of a curve of double curvature. Osculating circle. Application to the helix.

Radii of curvature of normal sections of a surface. Maximum and minimum radii. Relations between these and that of any section, normal or oblique.

Use of the indicatrix for the demonstration of the preceding results Conjugate tangents. Definition of the lines of curvature. Lines of curvature of certain simple surfaces. Surface of revolution. Developable surfaces. Differential equation of lines of curvature in general.

LESSON 28. *Cylindrical, Conical, Conoidal surfaces, and Surfaces of Revolution.*

Equations of these surfaces in finite terms. Differential equations of the same deduced from their characteristic geometrical properties.

INTEGRAL CALCULUS.

LESSONS 29—34. *Integration of Functions of a Single Variable.*

Object of the integral calculus. There always exists a function which has a given function for its derivative.

Indefinite integrals. Definite integrals. Notation. Integration by separation, by substitution, by parts.

Integration of rational differentials, integer or fractional, in the several cases which may present themselves. Integration of the algebraical differentials, which contain a radical of the second degree of the form $\sqrt{c+bx+cx^2}$. Different transformations which render the differential rational. Reduction of the radical to one of the forms

$$\sqrt{x^2+x^2}, \quad \sqrt{a^2-x^2}, \quad \sqrt{x^2-a^2}.$$

Integration of the algebraical differentials which contain two radicals of the form

$$\sqrt{a+x}, \quad \sqrt{b+x},$$

or any number of monomials affected with fractional indices. Application to the expressions

$$\frac{x^m dx}{\sqrt{1-x^2}}, \quad \frac{dx}{x^m\sqrt{1-x^2}}, \quad \frac{x^m dx}{\sqrt{ax-x}},$$

Integration of the differentials

$$\text{F} (\log x) \frac{dx}{x}, \quad \text{F} \sin^{-1} x \frac{dx}{\sqrt{1-x^2}}. \quad x (\log x^n)\, dx, \quad x^m e^{ax}\, dx, \quad (\sin^{-1} x^m)\, dx.$$

Integration of the differentials $e^{ax} \sin bxdx$ and $e^{ax} \cos bxdx$.

Integration of $(\sin x^m.) (\cos x^n)\, dx$.

Integration by series. Application to the expression

$$\frac{dx}{\sqrt{ax-x^2}\,\sqrt{1-bx}.}$$

Application of integration by series to the development of functions, the development of whose derivatives is given; $\tan^{-1}x$, $\sin^{-1}x$, $\log(1+x.)$

LESSONS 35—38. *Geometrical Applications.*

Quadrature of certain curves. Circle, hyperbola, cycloid, logarithmic spiral, &c.

Rectification of curves by rectilinear or polar co-ordinates. Examples. Numerical applications.

Cubic content of solids of revolution. Quadrature of their surfaces.

Cubic content of solids in general, with rectilinear or polar co-ordinates. Numerical applications.

Quadrature of any curved surfaces expressed by rectangular co-ordinates. Application to the sphere.

LESSONS 39—42. *Mechanical Applications.*

General formula for the determination of the center of gravity of solids, curved or plane surfaces, and arcs of curves. Various applications.

Guldin's theorem.

Volume of the truncated cylinder.

General formula which represent the components of the attraction of a body upon a material point, upon the supposition that the action upon each element varies inversely as the square of the distance. Attraction of a spherical shell on an external or internal point.

Definition of moments of inertia. How to calculate the moment of inertia of a body in relation to a straight line, when the moment in relation to a parallel straight line is known. How to represent the moments of inertia of a body relative to the straight lines which pass through a given point by means of the radii vectores of an ellipsoid. What is meant by the *principal axes of inertia.*

Determination of the principal moments of inertia of certain homogeneous bodies, sphere, ellipsoid, prism, &c.

LESSONS 43—45. *Calculus of Differences.*

Calculation of differences of different orders of a function of one variable by means of values of the function corresponding to equidistant values of the variable.

Expression for any one of the values of the function by means of the first, and its differences. Numerical applications; construction of tables representing a function whose differences beyond a certain order may be neglected. Application to the theory of interpolation. Formulæ for approximation by quadratures. Numerical exercises relative to the area of equilateral hyperbola or the calculation of a logarithm.

LESSONS 46—48. *Revision.*

General reflections on the subjects contained in the preceding course.

ANALYSIS.—*SECOND YEAR.*

CONTINUATION OF THE INTEGRAL CALCULUS.

LESSONS 1—2. *Definite Integrals.*

Differentiation of a definite integral with respect to a parameter in it, which is made to vary. Geometrical demostration of the formula. Integration under the sign of integration. Application to the determination of certain definite integrals.

Determination of the integrals $\int \frac{\sin ax}{x} dx$, and $\int \frac{\cos bx \sin ax}{x} dx$, between the limits o and x. Remarkable discontinuity which these integrals present.

Determination of $\int e^{-x^2} dx$ and $\int e^{-x^2} \cos mxdx$ between the limits 0 and ∞.

LESSONS 3. *Integration of Differentials containing several Variables.*

Condition that an expression of the form $M\,dx + N\,dy$ in which M and N are given functions of x and y may be an exact differential of two independent variables x and y. When this condition is satisfied, to find the function.

Extension of this theory to the case of three variables.

LESSONS 4—6. *Integration of Differential Equations of the First Order.*

Differential equations of the first order with two variables. Problem in geometry to which these equations correspond. What is meant by their integral. This integral always exists, and its expression contains an arbitrary constant.

Integration of the equation $M\,d\,x + N\,d\,y = 0$ when its first member is an exact differential. Whatever the functions M and N may be there always exists a factor μ, such that $\mu\,(M\,d\,x + N\,d\,y)$ is an exact differential.

Integration of homogeneous equations. Their general integral represents a system of similar curves. The equation $(a + b\,x + c\,y)\,d\,x + (a' + b'\,x + c'\,y)\,d\,y = c$, may be rendered homogeneous. Particular case where the method fails. How the integration may be effected in such case.

Integration of the linear equation of the first order $\frac{dy}{dx} + P\,y = Q$, where P and Q denote functions of x. Examples.

Remarks on the integration of equations of the first order which contain a higher power than the first of $\frac{dy}{dx}$. Case in which it may be resolved in respect of $\frac{dy}{dx}$. Case in which it may be resolved in respect of x or y.

Integrations of the equation $y = x\,\frac{dy}{dx} + \phi\left(\frac{d\,y}{d\,x}\right)$. Its general integral represents a system of straight lines. A particular solution represents the envelop of this system.

Solution of various problems in geometry which lead to differential equations of the first order.

LESSONS 7—8. *Integration of Differential Equations of Orders superior to the First.*

The general integral of an equation of the m order contains m arbitrary constants.

(*The demonstration is made to depend on the consideration of infinitely small quantities.*)

Integration of the equation $\frac{d^m\,y}{d\,x^m} = \phi\,(x.)$

Integration of the equation $\frac{d^2\,y}{d\,x^2} = \phi\left(y, \frac{d\,y}{d\,x}\right)$

How this is reduced to an equation of the first order. Solution of various problems in geometry which conduct to differential equations of the second order.

LESSONS 9—10. *On Linear Equations.*

When a linear equation of the mth order contains no term independent of the unknown function and its derivatives, the sum of any number whatever of particular integrals multiplied by arbitrary constants is also an integral. From this the conclusion is drawn that the general integral of this equation is deducible from the knowledge of m particular integrals.

Application to linear equations with constant co-efficients. Their integration is made to depend on the resolution of an algebraical equation. Case where this equation has imaginary roots. Case where it has equal roots. The general integral of a linear equation of any order, which contains a term independent of the function, may be reduced by the aid of quadratures to the integration of the same equation with this term omitted.

Lesson 11. *Simultaneous Equations.*

General considerations on the integration of simultaneous equations. It may be made to depend on the integrations of a single differential equation. Integration of a system of two simultaneous linear equations of the first order.

Lesson 12. *Integrations of Equations by Series.*

Development of the unknown function of the variable x according to the powers of $x-a$. In certain cases only a particular integral is obtained. If the equation is linear, the general integral may be deduced from it by the variation of constants.

Lessons 13—16. *Partial Differential Equations.*

Elimination of the arbitrary functions which enter into an equation by means of partial derivatives. Integration of an equation of partial differences with two independent variables, in the case where it is linear in respect to the derivatives of the unknown function. The general integral contains an arbitrary function.

Indication of the geometrical problem, of which the partial differential equation expresses analytically the enunciation. Integration of the partial differential equations to cylindrical, conical, conoidal surfaces of revolution. Determination of the arbitrary functions.

Integration of the equation $\frac{d^2 u}{d y^2}=a^2\frac{d^2 u}{d x^2}$. The general integral contains two arbitrary functions. Determination of these functions.

Lessons 17—23. *Applications to Mechanics.*

Equation to the catenary.

Vertical motion of a heavy particle, taking into account the variation of gravity according to the distance from the center of the earth. Vertical motion of a heavy point in a resisting medium, the resistance being supposed proportional to the square of the velocity.

Motion of a heavy point compelled to remain in a circle or cycloid. Simple pendulum. Indication of the analytical problem to which we are led in investigating the motion of a free point.

Motion of projectiles in a vacuum. Calculation of the longitudinal and transversal vibrations of cords. Longitudinal vibrations of elastic rods. Vibration of gases in cylindical tubes.

Lessons 24—26. *Applications to Astronomy.*

Calculation of the force which attracts the planets, deduced from Kepler's laws. Numerical data of the question.

Calculation of the relative motion of two points attracting one another, according to the inverse square of the distance.

Determination of the masses of the earth and of the planets accompanied by satellites. Numerical applications.

LESSONS 27—30.

Elements of the calculus of probabilities and social arithmetic.

General principles of the calculus of chances. Simple probability, compound probability, partial probability, total probability. Repeated trials. Enunciation of Bernouilli's theorem (without proof.)

Mathematical expectation. Applications to various cases, and especially to lotteries.

Tables of population and mortality. Mean life annuities, life interests, assurances, &c.

LESSONS 31—32. *Revision.*

General reflections on the subjects comprised in the course.

II. DESCRIPTIVE GEOMETRY AND STEREOTOMY.

General Arrangements.

The pupils take in the lecture-room notes and sketches upon sheets, which are presented to the professor and the "répétiteurs" at each interrogation. The care with which these notes are taken is determined by "marks," of which account is taken in arranging the pupils in order of merit.

The plans are made according to programmes, of which the conditions are different for different pupils. The drawings are in general acccompanied with decimal scales, expressing a simple ratio to the meter. They carry inscriptions written conformably to the admitted models, and are, when necessary, accompanied with verbal descriptions.

In the graphic exercises of the first part of the course, the principal object is to familiarize the pupils with the different kinds of geometrical drawing, such as elevations and shaded sections, oblique projections and various kinds of perspective. The pupils are also accustomed to different constructions useful in stereotomy.

The subjects for graphic exercises in stereotomy are taken from roofs, vaults, and staircases. Skew and oblique arches are the subject of detailed plans.

FIRST YEAR.

DESCRIPTIVE GEOMETRY.—GEOMETRICAL DRAWING.

LESSONS 1—3 *Revision and Completion of the Subjects of Descriptive Geometry comprised in the Programme for Admission into the School.*

Object of geometrical drawing. Methods of projection. Representation of points, lines, planes, cones, cylinders, and surfaces of revolution. Construction of tangent planes to surfaces, of curves, of intersection of surfaces, of their tangents and their assymplotes.

Osculating plane of a curve of double curvature. A curve in general cuts its osculating plane.

When the generating line of a cylinder or a cone becomes a tangent to the directrix, the cylinder or cone in general has an edge of regression along this generating line. The osculating plane of the directrix at the point of contact touches the surface along this edge.

Projections of curves of double curvature; infinite branches and their assymplotes, inflections, nodes, cusps, &c.

Change of planes of projection.

Reduction of scale; transposition.

Advantage and employment of curves of error; their irrelevant solutions.

LESSONS 4—6. *Modes of Representation for the Complete Definition of Objects.*

Pepresentation by plans, sections, and elevation.

Projection by the method of contours. Representation of a point, a line, and a plane; questions relative to the straight line and plane. Representation of cones and cylinders; tangent planes to these surfaces.

LESSONS 7—11. *Modes of Representation which are not enough in themselves to define objects completely*

Isometrical and other kinds of perspective.

Oblique projections.

Conical perspective: vanishing points; scales of perspective; method of squares; perspective of curved lines; diverse applications. Choice of the point of sight. Rules for putting an elevation in perspective. Rule for determining the point of sight of a given picture, and for passing from the perspective to the plan as far as that is possible. Perspective of reflected images. Notions on panoramas.

LESSONS 12—13. *Representations with Shadows.*

General observations on envelops and characteristics.

A developable surface is the envolop of the position of a movable plane; it is composed of two sheets which meet. It may be considered as generated by a straight line, which moves so as to remain always a tangent to a fixed curve.

Theory of shade and shadow, of the penumbra, of the brilliant point, of curves of equal intensity, of bright and dark edges.

Atmospheric light: direction of the principal atmospheric ray. Notions on the degradation of tints; construction of curves of equal tint.

Influence of light reflected by neighboring bodies.

Received convention in geometrical drawing on the direction of the luminous ray, &c.

Perspective of shadows.

LESSONS 14—15. *Construction of Lines of Shadows and of Perspective of Surfaces.*

Use of circumscribed cones and cylinders, and of the normal parallel to a given straight line.

General method of construction of lines of shadow and of perspective of surfaces by plane sections and auxiliary cylindrical or conical surfaces.

Construction of lines of shadow and perspective of a surface of revolution.

The curve of contact of a cone circumscribed about a surface of the second degree is a plane curve. Its plane is parallel to the diametral plane, conjugate to the diameter passing through the summit of the cone. The curve of contact of a cylinder circumscribed about a surface of the second degree is a plane curve, and situated in the diametral plane conjugate to the diameter parallel to the axis of the cylinder.

The plane parallel sections of a surface of the second degree are similar curves. The locus of their centers is the diameter conjugate to that one of the secant planes which passes through the center of the surface.

General study of surfaces with reference to the geometrical constructions to which their use gives rise.

LESSON 16. *Complementary Notions on Developable Surfaces.*

Development of a developable surface; construction of transformed curves and their tangents. Developable surface; an envelop of the osculating planes of a curve. The osculating plane of a curve at a given point may be constructed by considering it as the edge of regression of a developable surface; this construction presents some uncertainty in practice. Notions on the helix and the developable helicoid.

Approximate development of a segment of an undevelopable surface.

LESSONS 17—18. *Hyperbolic Paraboloid.*

Double mode of generation of the paraboloid by straight lines; plane-directers; tangent planes, vertex, axis, principal planes; representation of this surface. Construction of the tangent plane parallel to a given plane. Construction of plane sections and of curves of contact, of cones, and circumscribed cylinders.

Scalene paraboloid. Isosceles paraboloid.

Identity of the paraboloid with one of the five surfaces of the second degree studied in analytical geometry.

Re-statement without demonstration of the properties of this surface found by analysis, principally as regards its generation by the conic sections.

LESSONS 19—20. *General Properties of Warped or Ruled Surfaces.*

Principal modes of generation of warped surfaces. When two warped surfaces touch in three points of a common generatrix, they touch each other in every point of this straight line. Every plane passing through a generatrix touches the surface at one point in this line. The tangent plane at infinity is the plane-directer to all the paraboloids of "raccordement."

Construction of the tangent planes and curves of contact of circumscribed cones and cylinders. When two infinitely near generatrices of a warped surface are in the same plane, all the curves of contact of the circumscribed cones and cylinders pass through their point of concourse.

The normals to a warped surface along a generatrix form an isosceles paraboloid. The name of central point of a generatrix is given to the point where it is met by the straight line upon which is measured its shortest distance from the adjoining generatrix. The locus of these points forms the line of striction of the surface. The vertex of the normal paraboloid along a generating line is situated at the central point. If the point of contact of a plane touching a warped surface moves along a generatrix, beginning from the central point, the tangent of the angle which the tangent plane makes with its primitive position is proportional to the length described by the point of contact. The tangent plane at the central point is perpendicular to the tangent plane at infinity upon the same generatrix. Construction of the line of striction by aid of this property.

LESSONS 21—22. *Ruled Surfaces with plane-divecters Conoids.*

The plane-directer of the surface is also so to all the paraboloids of "raccordement." Construction of the tangent planes and curves of contact of the circumscribed cones and cylinders.

The line of striction of the surface is its curve of contact with a circumscribed cylinder perpendicular to the directer-plane. Determination of the nature of the plane sections.

The lines of striction of the scalene paraboloid are parabolas; those of the isosceles paraboloid are straight lines.

Construction of the tangent plane parallel to a given plane.

Conoid: discussion of the curves of contact of the circumscribed cones and cylinders.

Right conoid. Conoid whose intersection with a torus of the same height, whose axis is its rectilinear directrix, has for its projection upon the directer-plane two arcs of Archimedes' spiral. Construction of the tangents to this curve of intersection.

LESSONS 23—25. *Ruled Surfaces which have not a Directer-Plane. Hyperboloid. Surface of the "biais passe."*

Directer-cone: its advantages for constructing the tangent plane parallel to a given plane, and for determining the nature of the plane sections. The tangent planes to the points of the surface, situated at infinity, are respectively parallel to the tangent plane of the directer-cone. Developable surface which is the envelope of these tangent planes at infinity. Construction of a paraboloid of *raccordement* to a ruled surface defined by two directrices and a directrix cone.

Hyperboloid; double mode of generation by straight lines; center; assymptotic cone.

Scalene hyperboloid; hyperboloid of revolution. Identity of the hyperboloid with one of the five surfaces of the second degree studied in analytical geometry.

Re-statement without demonstration of the properties of this surface, found by analysis, principally as to what regards the axis, the vertices, the principal planes, and the generation by conic sections.

Hyperboloid of *raccordement* to a ruled surface along a generatrix; all their centers are in the same plane. Transformation of a hyperboloid of *raccordement.*

Surface of the *biais passé.* Construction of a hyperboloid of *raccordement;* its transformation into a paraboloid.

Construction of the tangent plane at a given point.

LESSONS 26—28. *Curvature of Surfaces. Lines of Curvature.*

Re-statement without proof of the formula of Euler given in the course of analysis.

There exists an infinity of surfaces of the second degree, which at one of their vertices osculate any surface whatever at a given point.

In the tangent plane, at a point of a surface, there exists a conic section, whose diameters are proportional to the square roots of the radii of curvature of the normal sections to which they are tangents. This curve is called the indicatrix. It is defined in form and position, but not in magnitude. The normal sections tangential to the axes of the indicatrix are called the principal sections.

The indicatrix an ellipse; convex surfaces; umbilici; line of spherical curvatures.

The indicatrix a hyperbola; surfaces with opposite curvatures.

The assymplotes of the indicatrix have a contact of the second order with the surface, and of the first order with the section of the surface by its tangent plane.

A ruled surface has contrary curvatures at every point. The second assymplotes of the indicatrices of all the points of the same generatrix form a hyperboloid, if the surface has not directer-plane,—a paraboloid, if it have one.

Curvature of developable surfaces.

There exists upon every surface two systems of orthogonal lines, such that every straight line subject to move by gliding over either of them, and remaining normal to the surface, will engender a developable surface. These lines are called lines of curvature.

The two lines of curvature which cross at a point, are tangents to the principal sections of the surface at that point.

Remarks upon the lines of curvature of developable surfaces, and surfaces of revolution.

Determination of the radii of curvature, and assymplotes of the indicatrix at a point of a surface of revolution.

LESSONS 29—30. *Division of Curves of Apparent Contour, and of Separation of Light and Shadow into Real and Virtual Parts.*

When a cone is circumscribed about a surface, at any point whatever of the curve of contact, the tangent to this curve and the generatrix of the cone are parallel to two conjugate diameters of the indicatrix.

Surfaces, as they are considered in shadows, envelop opaque bodies, and the curve of contact of a circumscribed cone, only forms a separation of light and shadow, for a luminous point at the summit of the cone, when the generatrices of this cone are exterior. This line is thus sometimes real and sometimes virtual.

Upon a convex surface, the curve of separation of light and shade is either all real or all virtual. Upon a surface with contrary curvatures, this curve presents generally a succession of real and virtual parts: the curve of shadow cast from the surface upon itself presents a like succession. These curves meet tangentially, and the transition from the real to the virtual parts upon one and the other, take place at their points of contact in such a way that the real part of the curve of shadow continues the real part of the curve of separation of light and shade. The circumscribed cones have edges of regression along the generatrices, which correspond to the points of transition.

The lines of visible contour present analogous circumstances.

General method of determining the position of the transition points. Special method for a surface of revolution.

Lessons 31—34. *Ruled Helicoidal Surfaces.*

Surface of the thread of the triangular screw; generation, representation, sections by planes and conical cylinders.

Construction of the tangent plane at a given point, or parallel to a given plane. The axis is the line of striction.

Construction of lines of shadow and perspective: their infinite branches, their assymplotes. Determination of the osculating hyperboloid along a generatrix.

Representation and shading of the screw with a triangular thread and its nut.

Surface of the thread of the square screw; generation, sections by planes and conical cylinders; tangent planes; curve of contact of a circumscribed cone.

The curve of contact of a circumscribed cylinder is a helix whose *step* is half that of the surface. Determination of the osculating paraboloid. At any point whatever of the surface, the absolute lengths of the radii of curvature are equal.

Representation and shading of the screw with a square thread, and of its nut.

Observations on the general ruled helicoidal surface, and on the surface of intrados of the winding staircase.

Lesson 35. *Different Helicoidal Surfaces.*

Saint-Giles screw, worm-shaped screw and helicoidal surfaces to any generatrix. Every tangent to the meridian generatrix describes a screw surface with triangular thread, which is circumscribed about the surface, along a helix, and may be used to resolve the problems of tangent planes, circumscribed cylinders, &c.

Helicoid of the open screw, its generation, tangent planes.

Lessons 36—37. *Topographical Surfaces.*

Approximate representation of a surface by the figured horizontal projections of a series of equidistant horizontal sections. This method of representation is especially adapted to topographical surfaces, that is to say, surfaces which a vertical line can only meet in one point.

Lines of greatest slope. Trace of a line of equal slope between two given points.

Intersection of a plane and a surface, of two surfaces, of a straight line and a surface.

Tangent planes, cones, and cylinders circumscribed about topographical surfaces.

Use of a topographical surface to replace a table of double-entry when the function of two variables, which it represents, is continuous. It is often possible, by a suitable anamorphosis, to make an advantageous transformation in the curves of level.

Lesson 38. *Revision.*

Review of the different methods of geometrical drawing. Advantages and disadvantages of each.

Comparison of the different kinds of surfaces, *résumé* of their general properties.

Object, method, and spirit of descriptive geometry.

SECOND YEAR.

STEREOTOMY.—WOOD-WORK.

LESSONS 1—4. *Generalities.*

Notions on the mode of action of forces in carpentry. Resistance of a piece of wood to a longitudinal effort and to a transversal effort. Distinction between resistance to flexure and resistance to rupture. Beams.

Advantages of the triangular system, St. Andrew's cross.

LESSONS 5—8. *Roofs.*

Ordinary composition of roofs.

Distribution of pressures in the different parts of a girded roof.

Design of the different parts of roofs, &c., &c.

LESSONS 9—10. *Staircases.*

MASONRY.

LESSONS 11—12. *Generalities.*

Notions on the settlement of vaulted roofs. Principal forms of vaults, *en berceau*, &c., &c.

Distribution of the pressures, &c.

Division of the intrados. Nature of the surfaces at the joints, &c., &c.

LESSONS 13—15. *Berceaux and descentes.*

LESSONS 16—22. *Skew Arches.*

Study of the general problem of skew arches.

First solution. Straight arches *en échelon.*

Second solution: Orthogonal *appareil.* True and principal properties of the orthogonal trajectories of the parallel sections of an elliptical or circular cylinder. Right conoid, having for directrices the axis of the circular cylinder and an orthogonal trajectory. The intersection of this conoid by a cylinder about the same axis is an orthogonal trajectory for a series of parallel sections.

Third solution: helicoidal. Determination of the angular elevation at which the surfaces of the beds become normal to the head planes; construction in the orthogonal and helicoidal *appareil* of the curves of junction upon the heads, and the angles which they form with the curves of intrados. Cutting of the stones in these different constructions. Broken helicoidal *appareil*, for very long skew arches.

Helicoidal *trompes* at the angles of straight arches; *voussures* or widenings, which it is necessary to substitute near the heads at the intrados of an arch with a considerable skew; case where the skew is not the same for the two heads. Orthogonal trajectories of the converging sections of a cylinder.

Lessons 23—25. *Conical Intrados—Intrados of Revolution.*

Skew *trompe* in the angle. Suggestions on the general problem of conical skew vaulted roofs.

Spherical domes, &c.

Lessons 26—27. *Intrados, a Ruled Surface.*

Winding staircases, &c., &c.

Lesson 28. *Helicodial Intrados.*

Staircase on the Saint-Giles screw.

Lessons 29—31. *Composite Vaulted Roofs.*

Various descriptions of vaults.

Suggestions on vaulted roofs with polygonal edges and with ogival edges.

Lesson 32. *Revision.*

Spirit and method of stereotomy.

Degree of exactness necessary. Approximate solutions. Case where it is proper to employ calculation in aid of graphical constructions.

Review and comparison of different *appareils.*

MECHANICS AND MACHINES.

GENERAL ARRANGEMENTS.

The pupils execute during the two years of study:—

1. Various drawings or plans of models in relief, representing the essential and internal organs of machines, such as articulations of connecting rods, winch-handles and fly-wheels, grease-boxes, eccentrics worked by cams or circles giving motion to rods; the play of slides, &c.; cylinders of steam-engines, condenser, pistons, and various suckers; Archimedes' screw, and other parts of machines.

The sketches of the plan drawings are traced by hand and figured. The drawings in their finished state are washed and colored according to the table of conventional tints; they all carry a scale suitably divided.

2. A drawing of wheel-work by the method of development, and tracing the curves of teeth by arcs of circles from which they are developed. This drawing represents, of the natural size, or on any other scale of size considered suitable to show the nature of the partial actions only, a small number of teeth either in development or projection; the entire wheel-work is represented by the usual method of projection, where in drawings on a small scale the teeth are replaced by truncated pyramids with a trapezoidal base.

3. Finally, numerical exercises concerning the loss of work due to the prejudicial resistances in various machines, the gauging of holes, orifices, &c.

Models in relief, or drawings on a large scale, of the machines or elements of the machines mentioned in the course, assist in explaining the lessons. They are brought back, as often as found necessary, under the eyes of the students. When possible, lithographic sketches of the machines, or the elements of the machines, which ought to enter into the course, are distributed among the pupils.

The pupils, divided into sections, pay their first visit to the engine factories towards the end of their first year of study; they make one or more additional visits at the end of the second year.

FIRST YEAR.

PART I. KINEMATICS.—PRELIMINARY ELEMENTARY MOVEMENTS OF INVARIABLE POINTS AND SYSTEMS.

LESSONS 1—2.

Object of kinematics, under the geometrical and experimental point of view. Its principal divisions.

Re-statement of the notions relative to the motion of a point, its geometrical representation, and more especially the determination of its velocity.

Simultaneous Velocities of a Point and the Increments of its Velocities.

Ratio of the elementary displacement and the velocity of a point to the displacement, and velocity of its projection upon a straight line or plane. Use of infinitesimals to determine these ratios. Example:—Oscillatory motion of the projection upon a fixed axis of a point moving uniformly upon the circumference of a circle.

Analogous considerations for polar co-ordinates. Relations of the velocity of a point, of its velocity of revolution and its angular velocity about a fixed pole; of its velocity in the direction of the radius vector; of the velocity of increase of the area which this radius describes.

Simple Motions of Solids, or Rigid Systems.

1. Motion of rectilinear or curvilinear translation; simultaneous displacements, and velocities of its different points.

2. Motion of rotation about a fixed axis; relation of the velocities of different points to the angular velocity.

Geometrical notions and theorems relative to the *instantaneous center* of rotation of a body of invariable figure and movable in one plane, or to the *instantaneous axis* of rotation of a rigid system situated in space, and movable parallel to a fixed plane. Relation of the velocities of different points to their common angular velocity. Use of the instantaneous center of rotation for tracing tangents; examples—and amongst others—that of the plane curve described by a point in a straight line of given length, whose extremities slide upon two fixed lines. Rolling of a curve upon another fixed curve in a plane. Descartes' theorems upon the intersection of the normals at the successive points of contact: cycloids, epicycloids, involutes, and evolutes. Extension of the preceding motions to the instantaneous axis of rotation of a rigid system movable about a fixed point.

COMPOSITION OF MOTIONS.

LESSONS 3—6 *Composition of the Velocities of a Point.*

Polygon of velocities. Example of movements observed relatively to the earth. Particular cases; composition of velocities taken along three axes; composition of the velocity of a point round a fixed pole, and its velocity along the radius vector. Method of Roberval for tracing tangents.

Composition of the Simple Motions of a Solid System.

Composition of any number of translatory displacements of a solid. Composition of two rotations about two intersecting axes. Composition of any number of rotations about axes cutting one another at the same point; parallelopiped and polygon of rotations. Composition of two simultaneous rotations about parallel axes; case where the rotations are equal and of opposite kinds. Decomposition of a rotation about an axis into an equal rotation about any axis whatever parallel to the first, and a translation perpendicular to the direction of this axis. Direct and geometrical decomposition of the most general motions of a body into a rotation about, and a translation along, an axis called the *instantaneous axis.* Composition of any two motions whatever. Every movement of an invariable system is at each instant of time decomposable into three movements of rotation, and three movements of tranlation with respect to three axes, which are neither parallel nor lying in the same plane, but otherwise arbitrarily chosen.

Relative or Apparent Motions.

Relative motion of two points whose absolute motions are given graphically *à priori.* Trajectory of the relative motions, relative velocities, and displacements upon curves or upon the direction of the mutual distance of the two points; use of the parallelogram to determine its amount. Relative motion of a point in motion in respect of a body turning about a fixed axis; relative motion of two bodies which turn about parallel or converging axes, and in general of two rigid bodies or systems impelled by any motions whatever. How this problem is immediately reduced to that of the composition of given motions.

The most general continued motion of an invariable figure in a plane is an *epicycloidal* motion, in which the instantaneous center describes a curve fixed in relation to absolute space, and traces relatively to the proposed figure a movable curve, which is rigidly connected with that figure and draws it along with it in its motion of rolling upon the other fixed curve. Case of space or spherical figures.

ON THE ACCELERATED MOTION OF A POINT.

LESSONS 7—9. *Accelerated Rectilinear Motion.*

Re-statement of the motions acquired relatively to the acceleration in the variable rectilinear motion of a point. Brief indication of the solution of six problems arising out of the investigation of the laws of the motion in terms of the space, time, velocity, and accelerating force. For the most part these solutions may be brought to depend on exact or approximate quadratures. Numerical exercises.

Accelerated Curvilinear Motions.

Re-statement of the notions acquired relative to the composition of accelerating forces; the resulting acceleration, the normal and tangential acceleration animating a point in motion on a curve. The total acceleration of a point upon an axis or plane is the projection upon this axis or plane of the acceleration of the moving body in space. In uniform curvilinear motion the total or resultant acceleration becomes normal to the curve. Particular case of the circle; value of the normal acceleration in terms of the velocity of revolution or the angular velocity of the radius vector. Case of any curve whatever; geometrical expression of the total or resultant acceleration.

Accelerated Compound and Relative Motions.

Geometrical investigation of the simple and compound accelerations arising out of the hypothesis in which the motion of any system of points whatever is referred to another system of invariable form, but also in motion, Geometrical and elementary explanations of the results obtained by means of the transformation of co-ordinates.

Examples or Exercises chosen from among the following Questions:—

Projection of circular and uniform motion upon a fixed straight line or plane; motion of a circle which rolls uniformly on a straight line; comparison of the motions of the planets relatively to each other, treating them as circular and uniform: comparison of the accelerating force on the moon with that of bodies which fall to the earth.

GEOMETRICAL THEORY AND APPLICATION OF MECHANISMS OR CONTRIVANCES FOR THE TRANSFORMATION OF MOTION.

Lessons 10—19.

Succinct notions on the classification of elementary motions and organs for transmission of motion in machines after Monge and Hachette, Lanz and Bétancourt.

The most essential details upon this subject are set forth in the following order, and made clear by outline drawings previously distributed among the pupils.

Organs fitted to regulate the direction of the circular or rectilinear motion of certain pieces.

Axle; trunnions, gudgeons; pivots and bearings; couplings of axes; adjustment of wheels and of their arms. Joints with hinges, &c.; sheaves and pulleys; chains, ropes, and straps; means of securing them to the necks. Grooves and tongue-pieces. Eyelet-holes sliding along rectilinear or curvilinear rods. Advantages and disadvantages of these different systems of guides under the point of view of accuracy.

Rapid indication of some of their applications to drawbridges and to the movable frames or wagons of saw-works and railways.

Transmission at a Distance of Rectilinear Motion in a determinate Direction and Ratio.

Inclined plane or wedge guiding a vertical rod. Wedge applied to presses. Rods, winch-handles, &c. Disposition of drums or pulleys in the same plane or in different planes; geometrical problem on this subject. Fixed and movable pulleys. Blocks to pulleys. Simple and differential wheel and axle moved by cords. Transmission through a liquid. Ratios of velocities in these different organs.

Direct Transformation of circular progressive motion into progressive and intermittent rectilinear motion.

Rod conducted between guides: 1°, by the simple contact of a wheel; 2°, by cross-straps or chains; 3°, by a projecting cam; 4°, by means of a helicoidal groove set upon the cylindrical axis of the wheel. To-and-fro movement, and heart-shaped or continuous cam, waves, and eccentrics. Simple screw and nut. Left and right handed screws; differential screw of Prony, called the micrometric screw. Ratio of the velocities in these different organs.

The example of the cam and pile-driver will be particularly insisted upon; 1°, in the case where this cam and the extremity of the rod have any continuous form given by a simple geometrical drawing; 2°, in the case where this form is defined geometrically by the condition, that the velocity is to be transmitted in an invariable ratio, as takes place for cams in the form of epicycloids or involutes of circles.

Transformation of a circular progressive motion into another similar to the first.

1°, by contact of cylinders or cones, the two axes being situated in the same plane; 2°, by straps, cords, or endless chains, the axes being in the same situation; 3°, by cams, teeth, and grooves, at very slight intervals; 4°, by the Dutch or universal joint. Case, where the axes are not situated in the same plane; use of an intermediate axis with beveled wheels or a train of pulleys; idea of White or Hooke's joint in its improved form. Endless screw specially employed in the case of two axes at right angles to one another. Combinations or groupings of wheels. Idea of differential wheels. Relations of velocities in the most important of these systems of transmission.

Transformation of circular progressive Motion into rectilinear or alternating circular motion.

Ordinary circular eccentric. Eccentrics with closed waves or cams. Examples and graphical exercises in the class-rooms relative to the alternate action of the traveling frames of saw-mills, of the slides or entrance valves of steam-engines. Cams for working hammers and bellows.

Transformation of alternating circular motion into alternating rectilinear motion, or into intermittent and progressive circular motion.

Pump rods with or without circular sectors, &c. Examples taken from large exhausting pumps, fire-engines, and common pumps. Suggestions as to the best arrangement of the parts. Lagarousse's lever, &c. Application of the principle relative to the instantaneous center of rotation to give the relations of the velocities in certain simple cases.

Transformation of alternating circular or rectilinear motions into progressive circular motion.

The knife-grinder's treadle. System of great machines worked with connecting rods, fly-wheel, &c. Watt's parallelogram, and the simplest modifications of it for steamboats, for instance. The most favorable proportions for avoiding the deviation of piston-rods. Simplification of parts in the modern steam-engines of Maudsley, Cavé, &c. Variable ratios of the velocities.

Of organs for effecting a sudden change of motion.

Suspendors or moderators, &c. Dead wheels and pulleys, &c. Mechanisms for stretching cords or straps, and make them change pulleys during the motion. Brakes to windmills, carriages, &c., &c. Case where the axes are rendered movable. Means for changing the directions and velocity of the motions. Coupled and alternate pulleys; alternate cones; castors moving by friction and rotation upon a plate or turning-cone; eccentric and orrery wheels. Means of changing the motion suddenly and by intervals; wheels with a detent pile-drivers; Dobo's escapement for diminishing the shock, &c.

Geometrical Drawing of Wheel-work.

General condition which the teeth of toothed wheels must satisfy. Consequence resulting from this for the determination of the form of the teeth of one of two wheels, when the form of the teeth of the other wheel is given.

Cylindrical action of toothed wheels or toothed wheels with parallel axes. External engagement of the teeth; internal engagement. Particular systems of toothed wheels; lantern wheels, flange wheels, involutes of circles. Reciprocity of action; case where the action can not be rendered reciprocal. Pothook action. Details as to the form and dimensions given in practice to the teeth and the spaces which separate them.

Conical action of toothed wheels, or toothed wheels with converging axes. Practical approximate method of reducing the construction of a conical to that of a cylindrical engagement of toothed wheels.

Means of observation and apparatus proper for discovering experimentally the law of any given movement.

Simple methods practiced by Galileo and Coulomb in their experiments relative to the inclined plane and the motion of bodies sliding down it. Various means of observing and discovering the law of the translatory and rotatory motion of a body according as the motion is slow or rapid. Determination of the angular velocity, &c. The counter in machines. Apparatus of Mattei and Grobert for assigning the initial velocity of projectiles (musket balls.) Colonel Beaufoy's pendulum apparatus. Chronometrical apparatus for continuous indications by means of a pencil. Eytelwein's apparatus with bands, and its simplest modifications. Apparatus with cylinders or revolving disks. Use of the tuning-fork for measuring with precision very small fractions of time.

(The principal sorts of the apparatus above described are made to act under the eyes of the pupils.)

PART II.—EQUILIBRIUM OF FORCES APPLIED TO MATERIAL SYSTEMS.

LESSON 21.

Résumé of the notions acquired upon the subject of forces, and their effects on material points.

Principle of inertia, notion of force, of its direction, of its intensity. Principle of the equality of action and reaction. What is meant by the force of inertia? Principle of the independence and composition of the effects of forces. Forces proportional to the acceleration which they produce on the same body. Composition of forces. Relation between the accelerating force, the pressure, and the mass. Definition of the work done by a force. The work done by the resultant is equal to the sum of the works done by the components. Moment of a force in relation to an axis deduced from the consideration of the work of the force applied to a point turning about a fixed line. The moment of the resultant of several forces applied to a point is equal to the sum of the moments of the components. Corresponding propositions of geometry.

Lessons 22—25.

Succinct Notions upon the Constitution of Solid Bodies.

Every body or system of bodies may be regarded as a combination of material points isolated or at a distance, subject to equal and opposite mutual actions. Interior and exterior forces. Example of two molecules subject to their reciprocal actions alternately, attractive and repulsive, when the forces applied draw them out of their position of natural equilibrium. Different degrees of natural solidity, stability, or elasticity; they can only be appreciated by experience.

Equilibrium of any Systems whatever of Material Points.

General theorem of the virtual work of forces applied to any system whatever of material points. It is applicable to every finite portion of the system, provided regard be had to the actions exercised by the molecules exterior to the part under consideration. Determination of the sum of the virtual works of the equal and reciprocal actions of two material points. Demonstration of the six general equations of equilibrium of any system whatever. They comprise implicitly *every* equation deduced from a virtual movement compatible with the pre-supposed solidification of the system.

Theorem on the virtual work in the case of systems where one supposes ideal connections, such as the invariability of the distance of certain points of the system from one another, and the condition that certain of them are to remain upon curves either fixed or moving without friction.

Equilibrium of Solid Bodies.

The six general equations of equilibrium are sufficient as conditions of the equilibrium of a solid body. Theory of moments and couples.

APPLICATIONS.

Lessons 26—29. *Equilibrium of Heavy Systems.*

Recapitulation of some indispensable notions for the experimental determination of the center of gravity of solids when the law of their densities is unknown. Re-statement of the theorem relative to the work done by gravity upon a system of bodies connected or otherwise. In machines supposed without friction submitted, with the exception of their supports, to the action of gravity alone, the positions of stable or unstable equilibrium correspond to the highest or lowest points of the curve which would be described by the center of gravity of the system when made to move. Influence of defect of centering in its wheels, upon the equilibrium of a machine. Case where the center of gravity always remaining at the same height the equilibrium is neutral. Examples relative to the most simple drawbridges, &c.

Equilibrium of Jointed Systems.

Equilibrium of the funicular polygon deduced from direct geometrical considerations: Varignon's theorem giving the law of the tensions by another polygon whose sides are parallel and proportional to the forces acting upon the vertices of the funicular polygon. Case of suspension bridges; investigation of the curve which defines the boundary of the suspension chain; tensions at the extremities.

Equilibrium of systems of jointed rigid bodies without friction. Determination of the pressure upon the supports and the mutual actions at the joints.

Equilibrium and stability of solid bodies submitted to the action of stretching or compressing forces.

Permanent resistance and limiting resistance of prisms to longitudinal extension and compression. Equilibrium and stability of a heavy solid placed upon a horizontal plane and submitted to the action of forces which tend to overset it. Resultant pressure and mean pressure; hypothetical distribution of the elements of the pressure on the base of support. Conditions of stability, regard being had to the limit of resistance of solid materials, co-efficient of stability deduced from it.

PART III.—ON THE WORK DONE BY FORCES IN MACHINES.

LESSONS 30—39. *General Notions.*

Principle of work in the motion of a material point. Extension of this principle to the case of any material system whatever in motion. Considerations relative to machanical work in various operations, such as the lifting of weights, sawing, planing, &c. It is the true measure of the productive activity of forces in industrial works. It may always be calculated either rigorously or approximately when the mathematical or experimental law which connects the force with the spaces described is given. Uniform work, periodical work, mean work, for the unit of time. Horse-power unit. Examples and various exercises, such as the calculation of the work corresponding to the elasticity of gases on the hypothesis of Mariotte's law, the elongation of a metallic prism, &c.

Dynamometrical Apparatus.

Dynamometer of traction by a band or rotating disc or register. Dynamometer of rotation with simple spring, with band or register. Dynamometer of rotation with multiple springs and with register for the axles of powerful machines. Improved indicator of Watt.

(These pieces of apparatus are made to act under the eyes of the pupils.)

Work of Animal Prime Movers upon Machines.

Results of experience as to the values of the daily work which animal motors can supply under different circumstances without exceeding the fatigue which sleep and nourishment are capable of repairing.

Theory of the Transmission of Work in Machines.

Principal resistance. Secondary resistances. Two manners in which bodies perform the duty of motors. Ratio of work done to work expended always inferior to unity. Different parts of machines; receiver; organs of transmission; tools as machines.

Calculation of the Work due to the passive resistances in machines.

Résumé of the notions previously acquired on friction. Application to the inclined plane, to the printing-press, to guides or grooves, to the screw with a square thread; different cases of uniform motion being impossible under the action of forces of given directions. Friction of trunnions, pivots, eccentrics, and insertions of winch-handles. Prony's dynamometrical brake; conditions of its application. Resistance to rolling; its laws according to experiment. Use of rollers and friction-wheels; their practical inconveniences.

Mixed friction of toothed wheels; the Dobo escapement: friction of the teeth in the endless screw.

Stiffness and friction of cords. Results of experience. Friction of cords and straps running round drums. Different applications; brakes; transmission by cords, endless straps, or chains.

Examples and exercises; effects of passive resistances in the capstan, the crane, pulleys, &c.

LESSON 40. *Revision.*

SECOND YEAR.

PART I.—DYNAMICS.—DYNAMICS OF A MATERIAL POINT.

LESSONS 1—2. *Completion of the Notions acquired on this Subject.*

Differential equations of the motion of a material point submitted to the continued action of one or more forces. The acceleration of the projection of a point upon any axis or plane is due to the projection of the forces on this axis or plane. The acceleration along the trajectory is due to the tangential force. Relation of the curvature to the centripetal force. Introduction of the force of inertia into the preceding enunciations.

The increase of the quantity of motion projected upon an axis or taken along the trajectory is equal to the impulsion of the projected resultant, or to that of the tangential force. The total impulsion of a force is got by methods of calculation and of experiment analogous to those which relate to *work.* The increase of the moment of the quantity of motion in relation to any axis is equal to the total moment of the impulsions of the forces during the same interval of time; direct geometrical demonstration of this theorem. In decomposing the velocity of the moving body into a velocity in the plane passing through the axis of the moments, and a velocity of revolution perpendicular to this plane, we may replace the moment of the quantity of motion in space by the quantity of motion of revolution. Particular case known under the name of the principle of areas.

Extension of the preceding theorems to the case of relative motions. Apparent forces which must be combined with the real ones that the relative motion of a point may be assimilated to an absolute motion. Particular case of relative equilibrium. Influence of the motion of the earth upon the accelerating force of gravity.

DYNAMICS OF ANY MATERIAL SYSTEMS.

LESSONS 3—8.

Principle or general rule which reduces questions in dynamics to questions in equilibrium by the addition of the forces of inertia to the forces which really act on the system. Equation of virtual work which expresses this equilibrium; it comprises in general the external and internal forces.

General Theorems.

These theorems, four in number, are founded upon the principle of the equality of action and reaction applied to internal forces. They may be deduced from the preceding rule, but the three last are obtained more simply by extending to a system of material points analogous theorems established for isolated material points.

General theorem of the motion of the center of gravity of a system. Particular case called *principle of the conservation of the motion of the center of gravity.*

General theorem on the quantities of motion and impulsions of exterior forces projected on any axis.

General theorems of moments of quantities of motion and impulsions of exterior forces, projected on any axis whatever.

General theorems of the moments of quantities of motion and impulsions of exterior forces about any axis. Analogy of these two theorems with the equations of the equilibrium of a solid, in which the forces are replaced by impulsions and quantities of motion.

Composition of impulsions, of quantities of motion, or the areas which represent them. All the equations which can be obtained by the application of the two theorems relative to quantities of motion and impulsions, reduce themselves to six distinct equations. Particular case called *principle of the conservation of areas.* Fixed plane of the resulting moment of the quantities of motion called *plane of maximum areas.*

General theorem of work and *vis viva.* Part which appertains to the interior forces in this theorem. Particular case called principle of the conservation of *vires vivæ*, where the sum of the elements of work done by the exterior and interior forces is the differential of a function of the co-ordinates of different points of the system. Application of the theorem of work to the stability of the equilibrium of heavy systems.

Extension of the preceding theorems to the case of relative motions. Particular case of relative equilibrium. Motion of any material system relative to axes always passing through the center of gravity, and moving parallel to themselves. Invariable plane of Laplace. Relation between the absolute *vis viva* of a material system, and that which would be due to its motion, referred to the system of movable axes above indicated.

Examples and Applications.

The following examples, amongst others, to be taken as applications or subjects of exercises relative to the general principles which precede.

Walking. Recoil of guns. Eolypile. Flight of rockets.

Pressure of fluid veins, resistance of mediums, &c. Direct collision of bodies more or less hard, elastic, or penetrable. Exchange of quantities of motion. Loss of *vis viva* under different hypotheses. Influence of vibrations and permanent molecular displacements.

Pile driving; advantage of large rammers. Comparison of effects of the shocks and of simple pressures due to the weight of the construction. Oblique collision, and ricochet. Data furnished by experiment.

Oscillations of a vertical elastic prism suspended to a fixed point, and loaded with a weight, neglecting the inertia, and the weight of the material parts of this prism. Case of a sudden blow. What is meant by the "*resistance vive*" of a prism to rupture? Results of experiments.

Work developed by powder upon projectiles, estimated according to the *vis viva* which it impresses on them, as well as upon the gun and the gases upon hypothesis of a mean velocity.

SPECIAL DYNAMICS OF SOLID BODIES.

LESSONS 9—12. *Simple Rotation of an invariable Solid about its Axis.*

In applying to this case the first general rule of dynamics, the theorem of the moments of the quantities of motion, and the theorem of work, we are led to the notion of the moment of inertia; explanation of the origin of this name. The angular acceleration is equal to the sum of the moments of the exterior forces divided by the moment of inertia about the axis of rotation. Sum of the moments of the quantities of motion relative to this axis. *Vis viva* of a solid simply turning about an axis. What is meant by *radius of gyration?*

Remind of the geometrical properties of moments of inertia, of the ellipsoid which represents them, of the principal axes at any point, of those which are referred to the center of gravity.

Pressure which a rotating body exercises on its supports. Reduction of the centrifugal and tangential forces of inertia to a force which is the force of inertia of the entire mass accumulated at the center of gravity, and a couple.

Particular case where the forces of inertia have a single resultant; different examples. Center of percussion. Compound pendulum; length of the corresponding simple pendulum. Center of oscillation; reciprocity of the centers or axes of suspension and oscillation. Pressure upon the axis. Influence of the medium; experience proves that the resistance, varying with the velocity, changes the extent of the oscillations, but does not sensibly affect the time. Experimental determination of the center of oscillation and the moment of inertia about an axis.

Motion of an invariable Solid subject to certain Forces.

General notions on this subject. Motion of the center of gravity; motion of rotation about this point.

LESSONS 13—19. *Various Applications.*

Motion of a homogeneous sphere or cylinder rolling upon an inclined plane, taking friction into account.

Motion of a pulley with its axis horizontal, solicited by two weights suspended vertically to a thread or fine string passing round the neck of the pulley, the axle of which rests upon movable wheels. Atwood's machine serving to demonstrate the laws of the communication of motion.

Motion of a horizontal wheel and axle acted on by a weight suspended vertically to a cord rolled round the axle, or upon a drum with the same axis, and presenting an eccentric mass. To take account of the variable friction of the bearings, and the stiffness of the cord, with recourse, if necessary, to approximation by quadratures. Oscillations of the torsion balance.

Balistic pendulum. Condition that there may be no shock on the axis. Experimental determination of the direction in which the percussion should take place.

Theory of Huyghen's conical pendulum considered as a regulator of machinery. How to take account of the inertia and friction of the jointed rods, as well as of the force necessary to move the regulating lever, &c.; appreciation of the degree of sensibility of the ball apparatus with a given uniform velocity.

Windlass with fly-wheel. Dynamical properties of the fly-wheel. Reduced formulæ for a crank with single or double action. Advantages and disadvantages of eccentric masses. Tendency of the tangential forces of inertia to break the arms. Numerical examples and computations.

Mutual action of rotating bodies connected by straps or toothed wheels in varying motion.

The wedge and punching-press. Stamping screw or lever used in coining, cams, lifting a pile or a hammer. To take account of the friction during the blow, and afterwards to estimate the loss of *vis viva* in cases which admit of it.

PART II.—SPECIAL MECHANICS OF FLUIDS.—HYDROSTATICS.

Lessons 20—22.

Principle of the equality of pressure in all directions. Propagation of the pressures from the surface to the interior of a fluid, and upon the sides of the vessel. Equations of equilibrium for any set of forces. Pressure exerted in the containing orifices. Measure of the pressure upon a plain portion of surface inclined or vertical (sluice-gate, embankments, &c.) Center of push or pressure. Pressure against the surfaces of a cylindrical tube. Effect, and resistance to oppose to the pressure. Manometer and piezometer. Equilibrium of a body plunged in a heavy fluid or floating at its surface. Stability of floating bodies. Metacenter. Laws of the pressure in the different atmospheric strata.

HYDRAULICS.

Lessons 23—27. *Flow of Fluids through small Orifices.*

Study of the phenomena which accompany this flow in the case of a thin envelop and a liquid kept at a constant level. Conditions of this constancy in the level, and the permanence of the motion in general. Motion of the lines of fluid; form; contraction; reversal and discontinuity of liquid veins. Fundamental formulæ for liquids and gases based upon the principle of *vis viva*, and Bernouilli's hypothesis of parallel sections or Borda's of contiguous threads. Torricelli's theorem relative to small orifices. What is called the theoretical expenditure, effective expenditure, and co-efficient of geometrical contraction. Co-efficient deduced from the effective expenditure. Its variations with the volume of the fluid contents, and the form of the inner surfaces of the reservoir. Results of the experiments of Michelotti, Borda, Bossut, &c. Phenomenon of adjutages. Venturi's experiments; influence of atmospheric pressure; loss of *vis viva;* reduction of the velocity and augmentation of the expenditure. Results of experience relative to the co-efficient of expenditure, the form and range of the parabolic jets, showing the initial *vis viva*, and the loss of *vis viva*.

Large orifices.—Sluice holes and floodgates; reservoirs or open orifices; expenditure; practical formulæ and results of experiment. Influence of the proximity of the sides and the walls. Arrangement to avoid the effects of contraction or the losses of *vis viva.*

Flow through conducting Pipes and open Canals.

Practical formulæ relative to the case of uniform sections of great length. Measure of the pressures at different points of a conduit-pipe. Expression for the losses of effect due to corners and obstructions. Flow of gases. Principal methods of measuring the volume consumed adopted in practice. Floats. Pitot's tube. Woltman's mill. Register mill in air or gas. Waste in such instruments. Modulus and scale for water-supply.

PART III.—DIFFERENT MACHINES CONSIDERED IN THE STATE OF MOTION.

LESSON 28. *General Considerations. Résumé of the Notions acquired on this Subject.*

Equation of *vis viva*, and transmission of work in machines, account being taken of the different causes of power and resistance. Physical constitution of machines; *receiver*, *communicators*, and *operator*. Influence of the weights, of frictions, of shocks, and any changes in the *vis viva.* Parts with continuous or uniform motion, with alternating or oscillating motion. Laws of the motion on starting from rest, and when the stationary condition is established. The positions to which the maximum and minimum of the *vis viva* correspond are those in which there is equilibrium between all the forces, exclusive of the forces of inertia. Advantage of uniform or periodic motion. General methods for regulating the motion; symmetrical distribution of the masses and strains; flys and various regulators. Brakes and moderators; their inconveniences. Object and real advantages of machines.

LESSONS 27—35. *Hydraulic Wheels.*

Vertical wheels with float-boards, with curved ladles, and with spouts. Figure of the surface of the fluid in these latter. Horizontal wheels working by float-boards, buckets, and reaction. Turbines. Description, play, and useful effects compared according to the results of experiment. Vertical wheels of windmills and steamboats. Screw propeller.

Windmills.

Description. Result of Coulomb's observations.

On the principal kinds of Pumps.

Special organs of pumps. Valves and pistons, force pump, sucking pump; limit to the rise of the water. Sucking and force pump. Dynamical effects. Indication as to the losses of *vis viva* and the waste in different pumps. Explanation of the hydraulic ram. Air vessel. Fire pumps. Double action pumps.

Various Hydraulic Machines.

Hydraulic press. Water engine. Exhausting machines; *norias;* under and overshot wheels; Archimedes' screw, construction and experimental data.

LESSONS 36—39. *Steam Engines.*

Succinct description of the principal kinds of steam-engine with or without detent. Effects and advantages of the detent. Condenser. Air Pump. Furnace and feeding-pump.

Variable detent. Formulæ and experimental results.

LESSONS 40—42. *Revision.*

Reflections on the totality of the subjects of the course.

IV. PHYSICS.—*FIRST YEAR.*

GENERAL PROPERTIES OF BODIES.—HYDROSTATICS.—HYDRODYNAMICS.

LESSONS 1—5. *Preliminary Notions.*

Definitions of physics. Phenomena. Physical laws. Experiments are designed to make them spring out of the phenomena. Method of induction. Physical theories; different character of the experimental and mathematical methods.

General Properties of Bodies.

Extension. Measure of lengths. Vernier. Cathetometer. Micrometer screw. Spherometer. Dividing engine.

Divisibility. Porosity. Ideas generally received on the molecular constitution of bodies. These conceptions, which are purely hypothetical, must not be confounded with physical laws. Elasticity. Mobility. Inertia. Forces; their equilibrium, their effects, their numerical estimation.

Weight or Gravity.

Direction of gravity Plumb-line. Relation between the direction of gravity and the surface of still water.

Weight. Center of gravity.

Experimental study of the motion produced by weight. In vacuum, all bodies fall with the same velocity. Disturbing influence of the air. Inclined plane of Galileo. Atwood's machine. To prove by experiment; 1° the law of the spaces described; 2° the law of velocities. Morin's self-registering apparatus with revolving cylinder.

Law of the independence of the effect produced by a force upon a body, and the motion anteriorily acquired by this body. Law of the independence of the effects of forces which act simultaneously upon the same body. Experimental demonstration and generalization of these laws. Law of the equality of action and reaction.

Mass. Acceleration. For equal masses the forces are as the accelerations which they produce. Relation between the force, mass, and acceleration. Collision.

General laws of uniformly accelerated motion. Formulæ.

Pendulum. Law of the isochronism of small oscillations and law of the lengths deduced from observation.

Method of coincidences or beats. Use of the pendulum as the measure of time. Simple pendulum; formulæ. Compound pendulum: the laws of the oscillations of a compound pendulum are the same as the laws of the oscillations of a simple pendulum whose length may be calculated.

Determination by means of the pendulum of the acceleration produced by gravity. This acceleration is independent of the nature of the body.

Remark that the formulæ for the motion of oscillation apply to the comparison of forces of any kind, that may be regarded as constant and parallel to themselves in all positions of the oscillating body.

Identity of gravity and universal attraction.

Measure of weights. Balance. Conditions to be attended to in making it. Absolute sensibility; proportional sensibility. Method of double weighing. Details of the precautions necessary in order to obtain an exact weight.

Different States of Bodies. Hydrostatics.

Solids. Cohesion. Transmission of external pressures.

Elasticity. The true laws of elasticity are unknown. Empirical laws in certain simple cases, and for a very small action. Elasticity of compression, extension, torsion. Experimental determination of the co-efficients of elasticity. Limits of elasticity. Limits of tenacity.

Ductility. Temper. Cold hammering. Annealing.

Liquids. Fluidity. Viscosity. Physical laws which form the basis of hydrostatics:—1° the transmission of external pressures is equal in all directions; 2° the pressure exercised in the interior of a liquid upon an element of a surface is normal to that element, and independent (as to amount) of its direction. These principles are demonstrated by the experimental verification of the consequences drawn from them.

Application to heavy liquids. Free surface, and surface *de niveau.* Pressure upon the parts of the containing vessel, and upon the bottom in particular; hydrostatic paradox; verificatory experiments. Haldat's apparatus. Hydrostatic press.

Application to immersed or floating bodies (principle of Archimedes;) verificatory experiments. (In treating of the equilibrium of floating bodies, the conditions of stability are not gone into.)

Superposed liquids.

Communicating vessels. Water level. Spirit level; its use in instruments.

Densities of solids and liquids. Anemometers.

Compressibility of liquids. Piezometer. Correction due to the compressibility of the solid envelop.

Gas. Expansibility. Other properties common to liquids and gases. Principle of the equal transmission of pressures in all directions. Weight of gases. Pressure due to weight (principle of Archimedes.) Weight of body in air and in vacuum. Aerostation.

Superposed liquids and gases.

Communicating vessels. Barometer.

Detailed construction of barometer. Barometers of Fortin, Gay-Lussac, Bunten. Indication of the corrections necessary.

Mariotte's law. Regnault's experiments.

Manometer with atmospheric air—with compressed air. Bourdon's manometer.

Law of the mixture of gases.

Air pump. Condensing pump.

Primary Notions of Hydrodynamics.

Toricelli's principle. Mariotte's vessel and syphon. Uniform flow of liquids. The same of gases.

Molecular Phenomena.

Cohesion of liquids. Adhesion of liquids to solids. Capillary phenomena. Apparent attractions and repulsions of floating bodies.

Adhesion of drops.

Molecular actions intervene as disturbing forces in the phenomena of the equilibrium and motion of liquids.

HEAT.

EFFECTS OF HEAT ON BODIES.

LESSONS 6—9. *Generalities.*

General effects. Arbitrary choice of one of these effects to define the thermometric condition of a body. Conventional adoption of a thermometer. Definition of temperature.

Dilating Effects.

Definition of the co-efficients of linear, superficial, and cubic dilatation. Approximate relation between the numerical values of these three co-efficients. The value of the co-efficient of dilatation depends upon the thermometric substance and the temperature selected as the zero point. It becomes nearly independent of the zero point when the co-efficient is very small.

Relation between volume, density, and temperature. Linear dilatation of solid bodies. Ramsden's instrument. Cubical dilatation of liquids. Dulong and Petit's experiments on mercury. Discussion. Regnault's experiments.

Cubical dilatation of solids and of other liquids when that of mercury is given.

Relations between the volume, density, and elasticity of a gas, and its temperature.

Cubical dilatation of gases. Experiments of Gay-Lussac, Rudberg, and M. Regnault. Advantage of varying the methods of experimenting in these delicate researches.

Methods based upon the changes of volume under a constant pressure, and upon the changes of pressure for a constant volume.

The disagreement of these two methods is due to deviations from the law of Mariotte.

The constancy of the co-efficients of dilatation previously defined is only approximately true.

Necessity of employing two different co-efficients of dilatation according as consideration is being had to the variations of volume to a given pressure, or of pressure to a given volume.

Empirical formulæ for the dilatation of liquids.

Graphical constructions.

LESSON 10. *Thermometers.*

Construction of thermometers. Mercurial thermometer. Details of construction. Fixed points. Different scales; their relation. Arbitrary scales.

Change which takes place in the zero point. Different precautions to be observed in using the mercurial thermometer.

General want of comparability of mercurial thermometers with tubes of different material.

Air thermometers. They are comparable with one another within the limits of the errors of experiment, whatever the nature of the tube employed. This property entitles the air thermometer to a preference for all accurate measures. Comparison of the air and mercurial thermometers.

THERMOSCOPE, DIFFERENTIAL THERMOMETER, PYROMETERS, BREGUET'S THERMOMETER.

LESSONS 11—13. *Changes of State produced by Heat.*

Exposition of the phenomena which accompany the liquefaction of solids and the solidification of liquids. Constancy of the temperature whilst the phenomenon is going on.

Sudden melting and freezing. Persistance of the liquid state beneath the melting point.

Influence of pressure.

Exposition of the phenomena which accompany the conversion of liquids or solids into vapor, and the inverse passage from the gaseous to the liquid or solid state. Constancy of the temperatures whilst the phenomenon is going on.

Influence of pressure.

Phenomena of ebullition in free space. Augmentation of the temperature and pressure in a confined space. Papin's digester.

Properties of vapors in spaces and in gases. Saturated vapors. Their tension does not depend upon the space which they occupy, but only upon their temperature.

Effects of a diminution or increase of pressure without change of temperature; the same without change of pressure. Effects of lowering the temperature in a limited region of space occupied by vapor.

Tension of a saturated vapor at the boiling point of its liquid.

Measure of the tensions of the vapor of water. Experiments of Dalton, Gay-Lussac, Dulong, and Arago, and of M. Regnault.

Tables of the tensions of steam. Empirical formulæ. Graphical constructions.

It is assumed that non-saturated vapors are subject to the same laws as gases.

APPLICATIONS. CORRECTION OF THE BOILING POINT IN THE CONSTRUCTION OF THERMOMETERS. BAROMETRICAL THERMOMETERS.

LESSONS 14—16. *Various Applications of the Laws previously established.*

A phenomenon can not always be separated from the accessory phenomena which concur with it in producing the final result. Necessity of corrections to render complex results comparable *inter se.*

Density of solids when regard is had to the temperature and weight of the gases displaced by them.

Precautions to be attended to in the experiments. Empirical formulæ for the density of liquids. Maximum density of water. The temperature corresponding to the maximum must be determined graphically, or by interpolation.

Corrections for measures of capacity, for barometric measures.

The uncertainty of the corrections can not, in any considerable degree, affect the densities of solids and liquids.

Density of gases. Biot and Arago's experiments. Special difficulties of the question. The uncertainty of the corrections may sensibly affect the results. Regnault's method.

The same method may be applied to the determination of the co-efficient of dilatation for gases.

Density of vapors. Definition founded on the hypothetical application of the same laws to gases and vapors. Formulæ. Experimental method of Gay-Lussac and of Dumas. Corrections. Comparison of the two methods. Necessity of conducting the experiments at a distance from the saturation point. Latour's experiments. Relations between the weight and volume of a gas, and its temperatures; between the weight and volume of a gas mixed with vapors, and its temperature. Various problems.

Hygrometry. Chemical hygrometry. Hygrometry by the dew-point. Psychrometry.

PROPAGATION OF HEAT.

Lessons 17—18. *Propagation at a Distance.*

Rapid propagation of heat at a distance, in vacuum, in gases, in certain liquid or solid mediums. Experiments which establish this.

Rays of heat. Velocity of propagation. Intensity of heat received at a distance. Intensity of heat received or emitted obliquely. Emitting power, power of absorption, reflection, diffusion. The emitting and absorbing power are expressible by the same number in terms of their proper units respectively.

Analysis of calorific radiations by absorption. Different effects of deathermanous or thermochroic medium. Different influences of increasing thicknesses of the combination of different mediums. Radiations proceeding from different sources, various effects of different mediums on these radiations.

The calorific radiations emanating from different sources, have all the characters of differently colored heterogeneous rays of light.

THEORY OF RADIATION AND OF THE DYNAMICAL EQUILIBRIUM OF TEMPERATURES. APPARENT REFLECTION OF COLD.

Lesson 19. *Law of Cooling.*

Definition of the rate of cooling. Many causes may conspire in the cooling of a body.

Cooling in space. Newton's law only an approximation. Experimental investigation of the true law. Method to be followed in this investigation. The velocity of cooling is not a *datum* directly observable. It must be deduced provisionally from an empirical relation between the temperature and the time. Preliminary experiments. Course of the definitive experiments. Elementary experimental laws.

Hypothetical form of the function which expresses the velocity of cooling. To determine by means of the preceding experimental laws the unknown form of the function which expresses the law of radiation. Relation between the temperatures and the times. This relation only contains data immediately observable, and may be verified *à posteriori.*

The contents which enter into the preceding relation depend upon thermometric constants and the nature of the radiating surface.

The contact of a gas modifies the law of cooling.

Lessons 20—21. *Propagation by Contact.*

Slow propagation of heat in the interior of bodies, in solids, liquids, and gases. Confirmatory experiments. Hypothesis of partial radiation. Theoretical law resulting from this hypothesis upon the decrease of temperatures in a solid limited by two indefinite parallel planes maintained at constant temperatures. Determination of the co-efficient of conductibility by the experimental realization of these conditions. This experiment determines a numerical value of the co-efficients; it is not of a nature to serve as a check upon the theoretical principles. Enunciation of the law resulting from the same theoretical principles upon the decrease of temperatures in a thin bar heated at one end.

CALORIMETRY.

Lessons 22—23. *Specific Heats.*

Comparison of the quantities of heat. The quantities of heat are not proportioned to the temperatures. Definitions of the unity of heat. General method of mixtures to estimate the quantities of heat. Experimental precautions and corrections.

Application of the general method of mixtures. Specific heats of solids and liquids. Law of the specific heat of atoms. Heat absorbed by expansion, restored by the compression of bodies. Experiments on gases. Specific heats of gases under constant pressure. Measure of specific heats of gases under constant pressure. Special difficulties of the question. Succinct indication of one of the methods. Specific heats to a constant volume.

Lesson 24. *Latent Heat.*

Component heat of liquids absorbed into the *latent* state during fusion, restored to the *free* state during solidification.

Influence of the viscous state. Latent heat of ice. Ice calorimeter; its defects.

Component heat of vapors, absorbed into the latent state during vaporization, restored to the free state during condensation. Measure of the latent heat of vapors. Regnault's experiments.

Empirical laws on the latent heat of vaporization.

Applications of Calorimetry.

Means of producing heat or cold; 1, by changes in density; 2, by changes of state. Freezing mixtures. Vaporization of liquids. Condensation of vapors.

Steam-boilers. Warming by hot air and hot water. Various problems. Sensations produced by a jet of vapor.

Different physical and chemical sources of heat; percussion, friction, chemical combinations, animal heat, natural heat of the globe, solar heat, &c. It will be remarked that mechanical work may become a source of heat, and heat a source of mechanical work.

STATICAL ELECTRICITY.—MAGNETISM.—STATICAL ELECTRICITY.

LESSONS 25—27.

General phenomena. Distinction of bodies into conductors and non-conductors. Distinction of electricity into two kinds. Separation of the two electricities by friction. Hypothesis of electric fluids. Effects of vacuum of gases and vapors of points. Electrical attractions and repulsions. Electrization by influence. Case where the influenced body is already electrized. Sparks; power of points. Electrization by influence preceding the motion of light bodies.

Electroscopes.

Electrical machines of Van-Marum, Nairne, Armstrong.

Condenser. Accumulation of electricity upon its surface. Leyden jar. Batteries. Electrical discharges. Effects of electricity.

Condensing electroscope. Electrophorus.

Velocity of statical electricity.

Atmospherical electricity. Phenomena observed with a serene sky. Electricity of clouds. Storms. Lightning. Thunder. Effects of thunder. Return-shock. Lightning conductor.

Different sources of statical electricity.

MAGNETISM.

LESSONS 28—30.

Natural magnets. Action upon iron and steel. Artificial magnets. The attractive action appears as if it were concentrated about the extremities of magnetic bars. First idea of poles.

Direction of a magnetized bar under the earth's action. Reciprocal action of the poles of two magnets. Names given to the poles.

Phenomena of influence. Action of a magnet upon a bar of soft iron; upon a bar of steel. Coercive force. Effects of the rupture of a magnetized bar. Theoretical ideas on the constitution of magnets. More precise definition of the poles.

Action of the earth upon a magnet. The earth may be considered as a magnet. Its action may be destroyed by means of a magnet suitably placed. Astatic needles. The magnetic action of the earth is equivalent to a *couple*. Three constants define the couple of terrestrial action. Declination. Inclination. Intensity. Measure of the declination; of the inclination.

Magnetic metals. Influence of hammering, tempering, &c. Methods of magnetizing. Saturation. Loss of magnetism. Influence of heat. Magnetic lines. Armatures.

Magnetization by the earth's influence. Means of determining the magnetic state of a body.

Measure of Magnetism and Electricity.

LESSONS 31—32.

Coulomb's balance. Distribution of magnetism on a magnetized bar; distribution of electricity at the surface of isolated conductors. Comparative discussion of the conditions of the two problems and the methods of experiment.

Laws of the magnetic attractions and repulsions. Law of electric attractions and repulsions. Comparative discussion of the conditions of the two problems, and the methods of experiment.

Determination of the law of magnetic attractions and repulsions by the method of oscillations.

Comparison of the magnetic intensity at different points of the earth's surface.

LESSONS 33—34. *Revision.*

Considerations on the totality of the subjects of the course.

SECOND YEAR.

DYNAMICAL ELECTRICITY.—GALVANISM.

LESSONS 1—2

Chemical sources of electricity. Experimental proofs. Arrangement devised by Volta to accumulate, at least in part, at the extremities of a heterogeneous conductor the electricity developed by chemical actions.

Pile. Tension at the two isolated extremities; at one single isolated extremity; at the two extremities reunited by a conductor. Continuous current of electricity. Poles. Direction of the current, &c.

Various modifications of the pile of Volta. Woollaston's pile, Münch's pile, &c. Dry piles; their application to the electroscope.

Principal effects of electricity in motion, and means of making the currents perceptible. Experiment of Oersted. Galvanoscopes.

Currents produced by heat in heterogeneous circuits. Thermo-electric piles. Thermometric graduation of thermo-electric piles.

Currents produced by the sources of statical electricity.

PROPERTIES OF CURRENTS.

LESSON 3.—1. *Chemical Actions.*

Definitions. Phenomena of decomposition and transference. Reaction of the elements transferred upon electrodes of different kinds.

Principles of electrotyping.

Causes of the variation of the current in ordinary piles; means of remedying this; Daniell's pile. Bunsen's pile.

LESSONS 4—8. 2. *Mechanical Properties.*

Reciprocal actions of rectilinear or sinuous currents parallel or inclined. Reaction of a current on itself.

Reciprocal actions of helices or solenoids. Continuous rotation of currents by their mutual action; by reaction. Analogy of magnets and solenoids. Electro-dynamical theory of magnetism. Action of magnets upon currents and solenoids. Action of currents upon magnets. Experiments of Biot and Savart. Continual rotation of a current by a magnet; of a magnet by a magnet.

Action of the earth upon currents; it acts as a rectilinear current directed from east to west, perpendicularly to the magnetic meridian.

Continual rotation of a current by the action of the earth.

Astatic conductors.

LESSONS 9—10. 3. *Magnetic Properties.*

Action of an interposed conductor upon iron filings.

Electro-magnets. Magnetization temporary or permanent. Principles of the electric telegraph. Electrometers. Reference to diamagnetic phenomena.

4. *Electro-motive Properties.*

Phenomena of induction by currents, by magnets. Phenomena of magnetism in motion. Induction of a current upon itself.

Induction of different orders.

Interrupted currents. Clarke's machine.

LESSON 11. 5. *Calorific Properties.*

Influence of the nature of the interposed conductor; of its section; of the intensity of the current. Unequal temperatures at the different junctions of a heterogeneous circuit.

6. *Luminous Properties.*

Incandescence of solid conductors. Spectrum of the electric light. Voltaic arc. Transfer of ponderable matter. Action of the magnet upon the Voltaic arc.

7. *Physiological Action of Currents.*

Some words on this subject. Muscles and nerves. Actions of discontinuous currents. Reotomic contrivances.

Reometry.

Compass of sines, of tangents. Experimental graduation of galvanometers.

The dynamical intensity of a current diminishes when the length of a current increases. Reostat.

Laws of the dynamical intensity of a current in a homogeneous circuit. Reduced length and resistance of a circuit. Specific co-efficients of resistance. Laws of the dynamic intensity of a current in a heterogeneous circuit.

The intensity of currents is in the inverse ratio of the total reduced length, and proportional to the sum of the electromotive forces. Formula of the pile. Discussion of the case of hydro-electric piles—thermo-electric piles. Conditions for the construction of a pile, with reference to the effects to be produced. Conditions for the construction of a galvanometer with reference to its intended application.

Laws of secondary currents in the simplest cases. The chemical intensity of a current is proportional to its dynamical intensity.

ACOUSTICS.

LESSONS 12—15.

Noise, sound, quality of the sound, pitch, intensity, *timbre.* A state of vibration in a solid, liquid, or gaseous body is accompanied with the production of sound.

The pitch depends on the number of vibrations. Unison. Instruments for counting the vibrations:—1st. Graphic method. 2nd. Toothed wheels. 3rd. Lever. Feeling of concord. Musical scale. Gamut. Limit of appreciable sounds.

Study of vibrating motions in solids. Vibrating cords. Vibrations transversal, longitudinal. Experimental laws. Sonometer.

Spontaneous division of a cord into segments. Fundamental sounds. Harmonic sounds.

Staight and curved rods. Transversal and longitudinal vibrations. Experimental laws. Division into segments. Nodes. Ventral segments. Membranes.

Plane and curved plates. The vibrations divide them into "*concamerations.*" Nodal lines. Harmonic sounds.

Study of the vibrations in liquids and in gases.

Theoretical ideas upon the propagation of a vibratory motion in indefinite elastic media, on an indefinite cylindrical tube. Waves of condensation of dilatation. Progressive nodes and ventral divisions. Laws of the intensities of sound. Direct measure of the velocity of the propagation of sound in water. Measure of the velocity of the propagation of sound in air. Formulæ without demonstration. Comparison of the formulæ with experiment.

Sonorous waves reflected in an indefinite medium.

Fixed nodes and ventral divisions. Sonorous waves reflected in closed and open tubes. Fixed nodes and ventral divisions; the vibratory state and density thereat.

Series of sounds afforded by the same tube. Effect of holes.

Sonorous reflected waves in rods. Series of sounds afforded by the same rod vibrating longitudinally. Indirect measure of the velocity of sound in gases, liquids, and solids.

Experiments on the communication of vibrating motion in heterogeneous mediums, on the general direction of the vibrating motion commuicated.

Intensification of sounds. Interferences. Beats. Different stringed and wind instruments. Means of setting them in vibration.

A few words on the organs of voice and hearing. Incompleteness of our knowledge on this subject.

OPTICS.

Lessons 16—17. *Propagation of Lignt.*

Propagation of light in a straight line. Rays of light. Geometrical theory of shadows. Velocity of light. Rœmer's observations. Laws of intensity of light. Photometers of Bouguer, Rumford. Intensity of oblique rays. Comparison of illuminating powers. Total brightness. Intrinsic brightness.

Reflection.

Reflection of light: its laws. Experimental demonstration. Images formed by one or more plane mirrors. To ascertain if a looking-glass has its two faces parallel.

Spherical mirrors. Foci, formulæ. Discussion. Images by reflection. Measure of the radius of a spherical mirror.

Definition of caustics by reflection. Definition of the two spherical aberrations in mirrors.

Woollaston's goniometer.

LESSON 18. *Refraction.*

Refraction of light in homogeneous mediums. Descartes' law. Experimental demonstration for solids and liquids.

Inverse return of the rays. Successive refractions. Indices of transmission in terms of the principal indices. Consequences of Descartes' law. Total reflection. Manner of observing it.

Irregular refractions. Mirage.

Refraction is always accompanied with the accessory phenomenon of dispersion.

Geometrical consequences of the law of refraction. Focus of a plane surface. Focus of a medium bounded by two parallel plane surfaces; by two plane surfaces inclined in the form of a prism.

Foci of a spherical surface; of a medium limited by two spherical surfaces. Lenses.

Formula for lenses. Discussion. Varieties of lenses. Optic center. Images. Measure of the focal distance of lenses.

Definition of caustics by refraction. Definition of the two spherical aberrations of a lens.

LESSONS 19—20. *Dispersion.*

Unequal refrangibility of the differently colored rays which compose white light. Analysis of heterogeneous light by the prisms. Newton's method. Solar spectrum. Homogeneity of the different colors. Second refraction of a homogeneous pencil. Experiment with crossed prisms. Precautions to be attended to in the experiments. The spectrum, obtained by Newton's method, differs from the spectrum produced at the focus of a lens placed between the prism and the picture, according to the method of Fraunhofer. Reasons of the comparative purity of this latter spectrum. Fraunhofer's lines. Different spectra of different sources of heterogeneous light. Marginal iridescence of a large pencil of natural light traversing a prism. Dispersion of light by lenses. Iridescence of focal images. Recomposition of light, by means of a prism at the focus of a spherical mirror or a lens, by the rapid rotation of a plane mirror, by the rotation of a disk with party-colored sectors. Compound colors.

Chemical and calorific radiations accompany luminous radiations.

Analysis of light by absorption. Characteristic action of transparent colored mediums upon different sorts of compound light. Different influences of increasing thickness. Effects of differently colored mediums upon heterogeneous light. Effects of differently colored mediums upon homogeneous rays separated by the prism.

LESSON 21. *Measure of the Indices of Refraction.*

Determination of the indices of refraction.

1. In solids. Measure of the refracting angles. Minimum of deviation. Measure of the corresponding deviation. Use of Fraunhofer's lines.

2. In liquids.

3. In gases. Special difficulties of the question. Experimental method. Biot's and Arago's experiments.

Any power whatever of the index of refraction diminished by unit is sensibly proportional to the density of the gas. Method of Dulong founded on this remark.

LESSONS 22—23. *Application of the preceding Laws.*

Rainbow. Different orders of bow.

Achromatism.

Achromatic prisms. Diasperometer achromatism of lenses; how to verify it. Definition of secondary spectra: their nature gives the means of recognizing, whether flint or crown glass predominates, in an imperfectly achromatic lens.

Instruments essentially consisting of an achromatic lens. Magic lantern; megascope; solar microscope; camera obscura; collimators.

Vision.

Summary description of the principal optical parts of the eye. They act like the lens of a camera obscura to form an image upon the retina. Distinct vision; optometers; short sight; long sight; spectacles.

Binocular vision; perspective peculiar to each eye; estimation of distances; sensation of solidity; stereoscope; estimation of magnitudes.

PERSISTENCE OF IMPRESSIONS; DIVERS EXPERIMENTS.

LESSONS 24—26. *Optical Instruments.*

Camera lucida. A lens is necessary to reduce to the same apparent distance the two objects seen simultaneously. Instruments to assist the sight; simple microscope; the magnifying power; distinctness; field; advantage of a diaphragm; it modifies the field and the brightness variously according to its position.

Woollaston's double glass; its advantages.

General principle of compound dioptrical instruments.

Compound microscope; experimental measure of its magnifying power, by means of the diaphragm, by means of the camera lucida.

Astronomical telescope; object glass; simple eye-glass. Necessity for a diaphragm; its place; the wires, their place; optic axis of a telescope. Parallax of the threads of the wires; magnifying power of the object-glass; of the eye-glass; field of view of a telescope.

Optic ring; different methods of measuring the magnifying power.

Distinctness of a telescope; night-glass.

Different distances of drawing out the eye-glass for short-sighted and long-sighted observers.

Different sorts of eye-pieces; positive eye-pieces; ordinary double eye-piece of the astronomical telescope. Ramsden's eye-piece; treble eye-piece of the terrestrial telescope. Negative eye-pieces; simple eye-piece of Galileo. Compound *ditto* of Huyghens; advantages and disadvantages of these different combinations; general principle of catadioptrical instruments.

LESSONS 27—29. *Double Refraction.*

Crystallized mediums do not all act upon light like homogeneous mediums.

Double refraction of Iceland spar: the extraordinary image turns round the ordinary image. The ordinary and extraordinary rays cross at the interior of the crystal.

Huyghens' construction; measure of the ordinary and extraordinary indices of refraction; attractive and repulsive crystals; a ray falling perpendicularly does not always bifurcate in a camera with parallel faces, nor in a prism. Definition of uniaxial and biaxial crystals.

The dispersion of the ordinary ray differs from that of the extraordinary ray.

The two rays are unequally absorbed in many colored mediums. Tourmaline.

Doubly-refracting prisms; their construction. Use of doubly-refracting prisms to measure apparent diameters, &c.

LESSONS 30—31. *Polarization.*

Successive refractions in doubly-refracting prisms. Special properties of the two rays emerging from the first doubly refracting crystal. Polarization by double refraction.

Reflection from transparent media polarizes the light partially or wholly according to the incidence. Brewster's law. Reflection of polarized light from a transparent medium.

Simple refraction partially polarizes the light. Many successive refractions polarize it almost totally. Piles of glasses.

Different methods to obtain a ray of polarized light, 1st, by reflection; 2nd, by simple refraction; 3rd, by double refraction, by eliminating one of the refracted pencils;—by a screen,—by total reflection, Nicol's prism, by absoption, tourmaline.

Distinctive characters of light completely or partially polarized.

LESSONS 32—34. *Theory of Undulations.*

Hypothesis of luminous undulations.

Vibratory state of a simple ray of homogeneous light. Vibratory state at the intersection of two simple rays of homogeneous light intersecting at a very small angle.

Experimental proofs in support of this hypothesis:

1st. Experiment with interferences, fringes. Their breadth is different for different colors; they give the various colors of the prism in white light. The alternately bright and dark sheets are hyperboloids of revolution. The measure of the fringes give the means of estimating the lengths of the undulations corresponding to different colors. .

2nd. Colored rings of Newton, observed by reflection, by refraction. Law of the diameters; these vary in absolute length for different colors. Variously colored rings with white light. Reflected rings with a white spot at the center.

The theory of the undulations does not apply merely to theses phenomena. Explication of the laws of reflection and refraction. Definition of polarization in the system of waves. Elementary application of double refraction and the polarization which accompanies it in uniaxial crystals when the face of the crystal is parallel to the axis, and the plane of incidence normal or parallel to this axis.

Chemieal and Calorific Radiations.

Chemical and calorific radiations are subject, like luminous radiations, to the laws of reflection, refraction, dispersion, double refraction, polarization, interferences.

LESSONS 35—36. *Revision.*

Considerations on the totality of the subjects of the course.

MANIPULATIONS IN PHYSICS.

The practical exercises which constitute the subject of this programme will be performed in part by the pupils under the direction of the professors and *répétiteurs*, in part by the professors and *répétiteurs*, with the coöperation of the pupils.

FIRST YEAR.

Use of various instruments, designed for measuring lengths. Experiments on weight with Atwood's machine, the inclined plane, Morin's apparatus, and the pendulum.

Some experiments on elasticity.

Various verifications of the principles of hydrostatics and hydrodynamics.

Construction of aerometers.

Construction of a barometer, of a manometer. Various verifications of the law of Mariotte.

Various experiments with the air-pump.

Determination the density of solids or liquids by different methods.

Construction of a thermometer.

Experiments on the dilatation of liquids and solids by means of the ordinary thermometer and by means of the statical thermometer.

Experiments upon the dilatation of air by various methods.

Experiments upon the tension of vapors by different methods.

Determination of the density of vapors and gases by various methods.

Leading experiments on calorific radiation.

Experiments on cooling.

Determination of specific heats, heats of fusion, heats at which bodies pass into vapor.

Cooling mixtures.

Use of the chemical hygrometer, the wet bulb hygrometer.

Rehearsal of the leading experiments on magnetism.

To magnetize a needle, to reverse its poles.

Rehearsal of the principal experiments of statical electricity.

Experiments verificatory of the laws of electricity and magnetism.

Use of compasses.

SECOND YEAR.

Experiments upon the chemical actions of poles.

Leading experiments in electro-dynamics.

Leading experiments upon the magnetic properties of currents.

Experiments on induction.

Experiments on the calorific and luminous actions of currents.

Quantitative experiments on the laws of currents.

Experiments on the propagation of sound; on the vibrations of rods of plane or curved plates, membranes, sonorous tubes.

Experiments on mirrors, plane or curved.

Experiments on lenses. Experiments on the decomposition of light by the prism—by absorption. Measures of the indices of the refraction of solids. Use of the magnifying glass and microscope; measure of the magnifying power. Use of different telescopes, with and without corrections. Measure of the magnifying power. Experiments on double refraction and polarization. Experiments on interferences and colored rings.

MILITARY SCHOOLS AND EDUCATION.

An account of the Military and Naval Schools of different countries, with special reference to the extension and improvement, among ourselves, of similar institutions and agencies, both national and state, for the special training of officers and men for the exigencies of war, was promised by the Editor in his original announcement of "*The American Journal and Library of Education.*" Believing that the best preparation for professional and official service of any kind, either of peace or war, is to be made in the thorough culture of all manly qualities, and that all special schools should rest on the basis, and rise naturally out of a general system of education for the whole community, we devoted our first efforts to the fullest exposition of the best principles and methods of elementary instruction, and to improvements in the organization, teaching, and discipline of schools, of different grades, but all designed to give a proportionate culture of all the faculties. We have from time to time introduced the subject of Scientific Schools—or of institutions in which the principles of mathematics, mechanics, physics, and chemistry are thoroughly mastered, and their applications to the more common as well as higher arts of construction, machinery, manufactures, and agriculture, are experimentally taught. In this kind of instruction must we look for the special training of our engineers, both civil and military; and schools of this kind established in every state, should turn out every year a certain number of candidates of suitable age to compete freely in open examinations for admission to a great National School, like the Polytechnic at Paris, or the purely scientific course of the Military Academy at West Point, and then after two years of severe study, and having been found qualified by repeated examinations, semi-annual and final, by a board composed, not of honorary visitors, but of experts in each science, should pass to schools of application or training for the special service for which they have a natural aptitude and particular preparation.

The terrible realities of our present situation as a people—the fact that within a period of twelve months a million of able bodied men have been summoned to arms from the peaceful occupations of the office, the shop, and the field, and are now in hostile array, or in actual conflict, within the limits of the United States, and the no less alarming aspect of the future, arising not only from the delicate position of our own relations with foreign governments, but from the armed interference of the great Military Powers of Europe in the internal affairs of a neighboring republic, have brought up the subject of Military Schools, and Military Education, for consideration and action with an urgency which admits of no delay. Something must and will be done at once. And in reply to numerous letters for information and suggestions, and to enable those who are urging the National, State or Municipal authorities to provide additional facilities for military instruction, or who may propose to establish schools, or engraft on existing schools exercises for this purpose,—to profit by the experience of our own and other countries, in the work of training officers and men for the Art of War, we shall bring together into a single volume, "*Papers on Military Education,*" which it was our intention to publish in successive numbers of the New Series of the "*American Journal of Education.*"

This volume, as will be seen by the Contents, presents a most comprehensive survey of the Institutions and Courses of Instruction, which the chief nations of Europe have matured from their own experience, and the study of each other's improvements, to perfect their officers for every department of military and naval service which the exigences of modern warfare require, and at the same time, furnishes valuable hints for the final organization of our entire military establishments, both national and state.

We shall publish in the Part devoted to the United States, an account of the Military Academy at West Point, the Naval Academy at Newport, and other Institutions and Agencies,—State, Associated, and Individual, for Military instruction, now in existence in this country, together with several communications and suggestions which we have received in advocacy of Military Drill and Gymnastic exercises in Schools. We do not object to a moderate amount of this Drill and these exercises, properly regulated as to time and amount, and given by competent teachers. There is much of great practical value in the military element, in respect both to physical training, and moral and mental discipline. But we do not believe in the physical degeneracy, or the lack of military aptitude and spirit of the American people—at least to the extent asserted to exist by many writers on the subject. And we do not believe that any amount of juvenile military drill, any organization of cadet-corps, any amount of rifle or musket practice, or target shooting, valuable as these are, will be an adequate substitute for the severe scientific study, or the special training which a well organized system of military institutions provides for the training of officers both for the army and navy.

Our old and abiding reliance for industrial progress, social well being, internal peace, and security from foreign aggression rests on:—

I. The better Elementary education of the whole people—through better homes and better schools—through homes, such as Christianity establishes and recognizes, and schools, common because cheap enough for the poorest, and good enough for the best,—made better by a more intelligent public conviction of their necessity, and a more general knowledge among adults of the most direct modes of effecting their improvement, and by the joint action of more intelligent parents, better qualified teachers, and more faithful school officers. This first great point must be secured by the more vigorous prosecution of all the agencies and measures now employed for the advancement of public schools, and a more general appreciation of the enormous amount of stolid ignorance and half education, or mis-education which now prevails, even in states where the most attention has been paid to popular education.

II. The establishment of a System of Public High Schools in every state—far more complete than exists at this time, based on the system of Elementary Schools, into which candidates shall gain admission only after having been found qualified in certain studies by an open examination. The studies of this class of schools should be preparatory both in literature and science for what is now the College Course, and for what is now also the requirements in mathematics in the Second Year's Course at the Military Academy at West Point.

III. A system of Special Schools, either in connection with existing Colleges, or on an independent basis, in which the principles of science shall be taught with special reference to their applications to the Arts of Peace and War. Foremost in this class should stand a National School of Science, organized and conducted on the plan of the Polytechnic School of France, and preparatory to Special Military and Naval Schools.

IV. The Appointment to vacancies, in all higher Public Schools, either among teachers or pupils, and in all departments of the Public Service by Open Competitive Examination. To a diffusion of a knowledge of what has been done, is doing, or is proposed to be done in reference to these great points, the NEW SERIES of "*The American Journal of Education*," will be devoted.

MILITARY EDUCATION

AN ACCOUNT OF

INSTITUTIONS FOR MILITARY EDUCATION IN FRANCE, PRUSSIA, AUSTRIA, RUSSIA, SARDINIA, SWEDEN, SWITZERLAND, ENGLAND, AND THE UNITED STATES.

IN A SERIES OF PAPERS PREPARED FOR

THE AMERICAN JOURNAL OF EDUCATION.

EDITED BY HENRY BARNARD, LL. D.

PHILADELPHIA: J. B. LIPPINCOTT & CO., 1862.

CONTENTS.

IV. RUSSIA.

V. SARDINIA.

VI. SWEDEN.

VII. SWITZERLAND.

VIII. ENGLAND.

IX. UNITED STATES.

PAPERS

For Teachers and Parents.

The Undersigned will issue a series of volumes under the general title of Papers for Teachers and Parents, edited by Henry Barnard, LL.D., devoted to a practical exposition of *Methods of Teaching and School Management* in different countries, with special reference to Primary and Common Schools, and Home Education.

The following volumes are now ready for publication:

I. American Contributions to the Philosophy and Practice of Education. By Professor William Russell; Rev. Dr. Hill, President of Antioch College; Rev. Dr. Huntingdon; Gideon F. Thayer, late Principal of Chauncy Hall School; Rt. Rev. Bishop Burgess, and others.

One Volume, 404 pages, Octavo, bound in cloth, $1.50; bound in half goat, $2.00.

II. Object-teaching and Oral Lessons on Social Science and Common Things, with various Illustrations of the Principles and Practice of Primary Education, as adopted in the Model and Training Schools of Great Britain.

One Volume, 434 pages, Octavo, bound in cloth, $1.50; in goat $2.00.

III. German Experience in the Organization, Instruction, and Discipline of Public or Common Schools; with Treatises on Pedagogy, Diadactics, and Methodology, by Professor Raumer, Dr. Diesterweg, Dr. Hentschel, Dr. Abbenrode, Dr. Dinter, and others.

One Volume, 520 pages, bound in cloth, $2.00.

IV. Educational Aphorisms and Suggestions—Ancient and Modern.

One Volume, 200 pages, Octavo, bound in cloth, $1.50.

V. Pestalozzi and Pestalozzianism, with sketches of the Educational views of other Swiss Educators.

One Volume, 480 pages, Octavo, bound in cloth, $2.00, in goat with Portrait $2.50.

The above volumes are now in press and will soon be followed by

VI. French and Belgian Methods of School Organization and Instruction. This volume will embrace the Subjects and Methods of Instruction in Mathematics in the Polytechnic School of France, the Routine of the Model Schools of the Brothers of Christian Teaching or Doctrine, and the authorized Manuals published under the sanction of the Minister of Public Instruction in France, and in Belgium.

VII. Dutch Schools—their organization, inspection, and teaching.

VIII. The Education of Girls, with an account of several of the best schools for girls, in different countries.

TERMS:

Orders will be received for the series, at $1.50 each.

The volumes will average over 400 octavo pages each, in long primer type, and in neat cloth binding.

F. C. BROWNELL, 25 *Howard Street, N. York City.*

GEO. SHERWOOD, 124 *Lake Street, Chicago, Ill.*

For Sale, Barnards		
	Educational Biography—Cloth,	$2.50
"	Reformatory Education and Schools,—Paper	1.50
"	Tribute to Gallaudet,—Cloth	1.50
"	Raumer's German Universites,—Goat	2.00
"	Normal Schools,	2.00
"	School Architecture,	2.00
"	National Education in Europe,	3.00

We give below a few notices of Mr. Barnard's labors and publications in the cause of public schools and popular education.

"I can not omit this opportunity of recommending the reports which have emanated from this source, as rich in important suggestions, and full of the most sound and practical views in regard to the whole subject of school education." *Bishop Alonzo Potter, in the School and Schoolmaster*, p. 159. *New York ed.*, 1842.

"The report, [for 1838,] contains a laborious and thorough examination of the condition of the common schools, in every part of the State. It is a bold and startling document, founded on the most painstaking and critical inquiry, and contains a minute, accurate, comprehensive, and instructive exhibition of the practical condition and operation of the common school system of education." *Kent's Commentaries on American Law. Note—Fifth Ed.* 1845. *Vol. II., p.* 196.

"The several reports of Henry Barnard, Esq., Secretary of the Board of Education—the most able, efficient, and best informed officer that could, perhaps, be engaged in the service—contain a digest of the fullest and most valuable information that is readily to be obtained on the subject of common schools, both in Europe and the United States. I can only refer to these documents with the highest opinion of their merits and value." *Do., Fifth Ed., p.* 196.

"His labors in Connecticut are characterized by great sobriety of thought, patient application to details, and the highest practical wisdom, as well as by the enthusiasm of a generous heart" *New York Review for April*, 1843.

"Here, [R. I.,] in the short space of four years, he created and thoroughly established a system of popular education, which, under the wise and careful administration of his successors in office, has become a model for general imitation." *Appleton's New American Cyclopædia, Vol. II., p.* 645.

"Henry Barnard, of Connecticut, has devoted his life to the promotion of education, and has contributed more than any other person in the United States to give consistency and permanence to the efforts of enlightened men in behalf of this great cause. He is eminently practical, and, at the same time, by his various writings, he has largely diffused, among all classes, true views of the nature and necessity of thorough instruction, especially in a country where the political institutions rest upon the people." *Recollections of a Life Time. By S. G. Goodrich, Vol. I., p.* 541.

"His name is associated, in both hemispheres, with those far-extending and successful efforts for the foundation of education, in the largest sense, and for the elevation, upon higher planes of life, of the great masses of men, which so illustrate our advancing civilization." *Dr. Humphrey's Life and Labors of T. H. Gallaudet.*

"I remember, with fresh interest, to-day, [opening of the State Normal School of Connecticut, in 1851,] how my talented friend, who has most reason of all to rejoice in the festivities of this occasion, consulted with me, thirteen years ago, in regard to his plans of life; raising, in particular, the question, whether he should give himself wholly and finally to the cause of public schools. I knew his motives, the growing distaste he had for political life, in which he was already embarked, with prospects of success, and the desire he felt to occupy some field more immediately and simply beneficent. He made his choice; and now, after encountering years of untoward hindrance here, winning golden opinions, meantime, from every other State in the republic, and from ministers of education from almost every nation in the old world, by his thoroughly practical understanding of all that pertains to the subject; after raising, also, into vigorous action, the school system of another State, and setting it forward in a tide of progress, he returns to the scene of his beginnings, and permits us here to congratulate him and ourselves in the prospect that his original choice and purpose are to be fulfilled. He has our confidence; we are to have his ripe experience." *Rev. Dr. Bushnell's Address on Opening of State Normal School in New Britain*, 1851.

"The career of Henry Barnard, as a promoter of the cause of education, has no precedent, and is without a parallel. * * * He stands before the world as a national educator. We know, indeed, that he has held office, and achieved great success in the administration and improvement of systems of public instruction in particular States. But these efforts, however important, constitute only a segment, so to speak, in a larger sphere of his efforts. Declining numerous calls to high and lucrative posts of local importance and influence, he has accepted the whole country as the theater of his operations, without regard to State lines; and, by the extent, variety, and comprehensiveness of his labors, has earned the title of the American Educator." *Massachusetts Teacher, Jan.*, 1858.

"Mr. Barnard, in his work on 'National Education in Europe,' has collected and arranged more valuable information and statistics than can be found in any one volume in the English language. It groups, under one view, the varied experience of nearly all civilized countries." *Westminster Review for Jan.*, 1854.

"It is an encyclopædia of educational systems and methods." *Massachusetts Teacher for Jan.*, 1858.

"The new school-houses in the United States, so well adapted to their objects, both in their exterior and interior, are visible marks of his zeal. His 'School Architecture' has been widely influential in America; and, since the Edinburgh Review called attention to its merits, the results of his suggestions are already manifest in England. "I have often had occasion to admire the magic influence of Dr. Barnard, his brilliant powers of eloquence, and his great administrative talents." *Dr. Wimmer's Die Kirche und Schule in Nord Amerika. Leipzig*, 1853.

"Dr. Barnard, by his writings on school architecture, has created a new department in educational literature." *Dr. Vogel. Leipzig.*

"This change, [in the school-houses and schools of Rhode Island and Connecticut, especially the gradation of schools,] is to be ascribed to the labors of Hon. Henry Barnard more than to any other cause. This gentleman has dedicated his remarkable abilities, for many years, to the improvement of common school education. The results of his labors may be discovered in almost every town in Connecticut and Rhode Island." *Dr. Wayland's Introductory Lecture before the American Institute of Instruction, for* 1854.

"Under his administration, common schools advanced rapidly. Gentlemanly in his address, conciliatory in his manners, remarkably active and earnest, he combines more essential elements of character for Superintendent of Education, than any other individual with whom it has been my fortune to be acquainted." *Hon. John Kingsbury.*

"For carrying out these measures of reform and improvement, an agent was selected, of whom it is not extravagant to say that, if a better man be required, we must wait at least another generation, for a better one is not to be found in the present." *Mr. Mann, in Massachusetts Common School Journal, for* 1846.

"There is no man whom our committee has consulted on this subject, for the last three years, who gives us so much satisfaction, who is so perfectly master of the subject, and so thoroughly practical in his views, as he. We regard him as deservedly the best and ablest guide on this subject in the whole country." *Hon. J. G. Hulburd, Chairman of Committee on Colleges, Common Schools, &c, in the Legislature of N. Y.*, 1842.

"The new system in Connecticut was most efficiently and beneficially administered under the auspices of one of the ablest and best of men." *Hon. Horace Mann, Oration on the Fourth of July, in Boston*, 1842.

"His task was to awaken a slumbering people, to tempt avarice to loosen its grasp, to cheer the faint-hearted, and awaken hopes in the bosom of the desponding. * * * We are glad to see such men engaged in such a cause. We honor that spirit which is willing "to spend and be spent" in the public service, not in the enjoyment of sinecures loaded with honors and emoluments, but toiling alone, through good report and evil report, alike indifferent to the flattery or the censure of evil-minded men, and intent only on the accomplishment of its work of benevolence and humanity. To that spirit is the world indebted for all of goodness and greatness in it worth possessing. The exploits of the conqueror may fill a more ambitious page in history; the splendors of royalty may appear more brilliant and dazzling in the eyes of the multitude; and to the destroyer of thrones and kingdoms they may bow, in terror of his power; but the energy and devotion of a single man, acting on the hearts and the minds of the people, is greater than them all. They may flourish for a day, and the morrow will know them not, but *his* influence shall live; and through all the changes and vicissitudes of thrones and kingdoms and powers on earth, shall hold its onward, upward course of encouragement and hope in the great cause of human progress and advancement." *New York Review for April*, 1843.

"We commend Mr. Barnard's Reports as valuable documents, ably and carefully prepared, and worthy the attention of all who feel an interest in the literature of education. * * We can not take leave of the subject, without recording our admiration of that singular disinterestedness which crowns his other good qualities. In point of fact, he has devoted his whole time gratuitously, for the last three years, to this interest. We record this fact with pride and pleasure, in the thought that, in this age of loud profession and restless self-seeking, an individual has been found, with the magnanimity to enter upon, and a resolution to persevere in, this modest course of self-sacrificing usefulness. Let the State of Connecticut look to it that she pays to such conduct its proper meed of gratitude and respect. One such man is worth a score of selfish politicians." *North American Review for April*, 1842.

"When I contemplate the picture of the immense mental labor accomplished in this way [by Mr. Barnard, in his labors to build up a system of public schools in Rhode Island;] when I think of what a mass of information has thus been spread, and how conviction has, as it were, been made to force itself upon every home, every head, and every heart; when I behold a people awakened to the consciousness of a great public evil, and in a manner driven out of their houses to correct it; when I see all this, I confess I am more affected by this crusade against dilapidated school-houses, inefficient schoolmasters, and faulty methods of instruction, than by many of the enterprises that are more lauded in history." *Siljstrom's Educational Institutions of the United States Stockholm*, 1852.

BARNARD'S EDUCATIONAL WORKS.

F. B. Perkins, of Hartford, Conn., and F. C. Brownell, (*No. 25 Howard Street,*) New York, will supply the trade or individuals with the following recent publications by Hon. Henry Barnard, LL.D.

PESTALOZZI AND PESTALOZZIANISM.

A Memoir of John Henry Pestalozzi, with selections from his Educational publications; together with Biographical Sketches of several of his Assistants and Disciples, with a portrait of Pestalozzi. 480 pages. Price per copy $2, strongly sewed, and bound in paper covers; and $2.50 in half morocco.

This volume gives the fullest account of the life and system of the great Swiss Educator which has appeared in the English language, and the most comprehensive survey of the work done by him and his Assistants and Disciples in any language.

THE GERMAN UNIVERSITIES.

Contributions to the History and Improvement of the German Universities. By *Karl von Raumer.* 250 pages. Price $1.50 per copy, strongly sewed, and bound in neat paper covers; and $2 bound in half morocco.

This first American Edition of the Fourth volume of Prof. Raumer's elaborate "*History of Pedagogy*" contains a comprehensive survey of the origin and peculiar constitution of the great universities of Germany; a minute and documentary account of the old customs and the modern societies of the students, of the Deposition, Pennalism, Nationalism, and the Burschenschaften; the Wartburg Festival, the assassination of Kotzebue, and the execution of Sand; together with a number of Essays on topics connected with college and university improvements, now agitated in this country as well as in Europe.

EDUCATIONAL BIOGRAPHY.

Memoirs of Eminent Teachers, Benefactors, and Promoters of Education, with twenty-one Portraits from engravings on steel by the best artists. 524 pages. Price for the illustrated edition, printed on thick paper, and bound in antique morocco, $3.50.

REFORMATORY EDUCATION AND INSTITUTIONS.

Papers on Preventive, Correctional, and Reformatory Institutions and Agencies, in different countries. 364 pages. Price per copy, bound in paper covers, $1.25; and in cloth, $1.50.

This volume contains a minute account of the Mettray Reform Farm School, (*Colonie Agricole et Penitentiaire,*) founded by Demetz, in France; of the Rough House (*Rauhe Haus,*) at Horn, near Hamburg; of the Reformatory Institution at Ruysselede, in Belgium; of the Red Hill, the Red Lodge, and Hardwicke Reformatories in England; with a comprehensive and practical survey of this class of schools and agencies in other countries.

TRIBUTE TO GALLAUDET.

A Memoir of Thomas Hopkins Gallaudet, with a History of Deaf Mute Instruction, and account of the American Asylum for the Deaf and Dumb in Hartford; with a Portrait and Selections from the Writings of Dr. Gallaudet. Second Edition. 224 pages. Price per copy, bound in cloth, $1.50.

THE AMERICAN JOURNAL OF EDUCATION.

The first Series of this "Encyclopedia of Education," embracing five volumes, each containing on an average over 800 pages, with thirty portraits of eminent teachers, educators, and benefactors of education, literature, and science, can now be furnished for $12.50 bound in cloth, and $15 bound in half calf or morocco.

Subscription to the same, for the year 1860, embracing four numbers, or two volumes, of 624 pages each, with 7 portraits, from engravings on steel by the best artists, $4, payable in advance.

Barnard's "School Architecture," and "National Education in Europe," will be furnished—the former for $2, and the latter for $3, per copy.

NORMAL SCHOOLS; and other Institutions, Agencies and Means, designed for the Professional Education of Teachers. By Henry Barnard, Superintendent of Common Schools in Connecticut. Hartford, 1851.

The above work was first published in 1847, to aid the establishment of a Normal School in Rhode Island, and afterwards circulated largely in Connecticut for the same object. It was enlarged in 1850, and published as one of a series of Essays which the author as the Superintendent of Common Schools, was authorized by the Legislature to prepare for general circulation in Connecticut, to enable the people to appreciate the importance of the State Normal School, which had been established on a temporary basis in 1849. The documents embraced in this treatise are of permanent value.

In addition to an account of the organization and course of instruction in the best Normal Schools in Europe and in this country, it embraces elaborate papers on the nature and advantages of Institutions for the professional training of teachers, by Gallaudet, Carter, Stowe Emerson, Everett, Humphrey, Mann, and others.

LEGAL PROVISION RESPECTING THE EDUCATION AND EMPLOYMENT OF CHILDREN IN FACTORIES AND MANUFACTURING ESTABLISHMENTS; with an Appendix on the Influence of Education. on the Quality and pecuniary value of labor, and its connection with Insanity and Crime. By Henry Barnard, L L. D. F. C. Brownell, Hartford. 84 pages.

This pamphlet of 84 pages, was prepared by the author in 1812, to fortify some recommendations contained in his Report as Secretary of the Board of Commissioners of Common Schools, for more thorough legislation to protect the health, morals, and souls of children from the cupidity of employers, and of parents, and at the same time to show how the productive power of the State could be augmented, and the waste of property, health and happiness, might be prevented by such an education as could and should be given in Common or Public Schools. The statistics and legislation on these subjects are of permanent and universal interest.

PRACTICAL ILLUSTRATIONS OF THE PRINCIPLES OF SCHOOL ARCHITECTURE. Third edition. By Henry Barnard. Hartford; F. C. Brownell. 1856.

This work is an abridgment by the author, of his large treatise on School Architecture, made originally for a Committee of the American Association for the Advancement of Education, and adopted as the first of the series of Essays prepared for general circulation in the state of Connecticut. An edition of 5000 copies was printed for circulation in Great Britain, at the expense of Vere Foter, Esq., of London.

CONNECTICUT COMMON SCHOOL JOURNAL; Vol. I, to Vol. VIII.

The Conn. Common School Journal was edited and published by Mr. Barnard, as Secretary of the Board of Commissioners of Common Schools, from Aug. 1838 to Aug. 1842; and as Superintendent of Common Schools in Conn., from 1850 to 1855. On the 1st of Jan. 1855, its publication was assumed by the State Teachers' Association.

REPORTS AND DOCUMENTS RELATING TO THE COMMON SCHOOL SYSTEM OF CONNECTICUT. Hartford: Case, Tiffany & Co.

This Volume is made up of different numbers of the Connecticut Common School Journal, which contain separate documents of permanent value. It makes a large quarto volume of 400 pages, in double columns, and small type. Price $1.00.

I.—DOCUMENTS CONNECTED WITH THE COMMON SCHOOLS OF CONNECTICUT FROM MAY, 1838, TO MAY, 1842.

REPORTS of the Board of Commissioners of Common Schools, for 1839, 1840, 1841, 1842
Barnard's Report—Legislative Document, 1838.
" Address of the Board of Commissioners of C. S. to the People, 1838.
" First Annual Report to the Board of C. C. S., 1839; Second do. for 1840; Third do. for 1841; Fourth do. for 1842.
" Report on Education in other States and Countries, 1840.
" " Public Schools in Boston, Providence, Lowell, Worcester, &c., 1841.
" Address on School-houses in 1839.
" Report on Public Schools of Hartford, 1841.
" Remarks on the History and Condition of the School Laws of Connecticut, 1841.
" Report on the Legal Provision respecting the Education and Employment of Children in Factories in various States and Countries.
" Letter to a Committee of the Legislature on the Expenses of the Board of Commissioners, 1841.
Reports of School Visitors in most of the Towns in Connecticut, for 1840 to 1842.
Summary of the Legislation of the State respecting Schools from 1647 to 1839.
Act to provide for the better Supervision of Common Schools, passed 1838.
Act giving additional powers to School Districts and School Societies, 1839.
Revised Common School Act, 1841.
Report and Act for repealing the Board of Commissioners, 1842.

II.—DOCUMENTS OR ARTICLES RESPECTING THE SCHOOL SYSTEM OF OTHER STATES AND COUNTRIES.

Condition of Public Education in Scotland, Ireland, England, and Wales, from various sources.
" " " Holland, by Prof. Bache, Cousin, and Cuvier.
" " " Prussia, by Prof. Bache, Cousin, Wyse, and Prof. Stowe.
" " " Duchy of Baden, and Nassau, by Prof. James.
" " " Austria, by Prof. Turnbull and Bache.
" " " Tuscany, from Qu. Review.
" " " Switzerland, from Journal of Education, and Prof. Bache
" " " Bavaria and Hanover, by Hawkins.
" " " Saxony, by Prof. Bache.
" " " Russia, by Prof. Stowe.
" " " France, by Mrs. Austin and Prof. Bache.
" " " Belgium, from Foreign Qu. Review.

III.—NORMAL SCHOOLS, OR TEACHERS' SEMINARIES.

History of Teachers' Seminaries.
Essays on, by Rev. T. H. Gallaudet.
Address respecting, by Prof. Stowe.
Account of in Prussia, by Dr. Julius.
" " France, by Guizot.
" " Holland, by Cousin.
" " Europe, by Prof. Bache.
" " Massachusetts, by Mr. Mann.
" " New York, by Mr. Dix.
Normal Seminary, Glasgow.
Teachers' Departments, New York.

State Normal School at Lexington, Mass.
Borough Road School, London.
Primary Normal School, at Haarlem, (Holland.)
Seminary for Teachers, at Weissenfels, Prussia.
" " Potsdam, "
Primary Normal School at Stettin.
" " " Brühl and Neuweid
Normal School at Versailles, France.
" " Kussnacht, Switzerland
" " Beuggen, "
" " Hofwyl, "

IV.—ACCOUNT OF PARTICULAR SCHOOLS.

Infant Schools.
Model Infant School, Glasgow.
" " " London.
Quaker Street Infant, "
Infant School in Lombardy.
" " Rotterdam.

Evening Schools.—Schools of Industry, &c.
Evening School in London.
School of Industry at Norwood.
" " Ealing.
" " Lindfield.
" " Gowers Walk.
" " Guernsey.
" " Warwick.
" for Juvenile Offenders, Rotterdam.

Public Schools of Various Grades.
Primary School at the Hague.
Intermediate School at Leyden.
Borough Road School, London.
Sessional School, Edinburgh.
High School, Edinburgh.
School for the Poor, Amsterdam.
Primary School, Berlin.
Dorothean High School, "
Burgher School, "
Higher Burgher School, Potsdam.
Lovell's Lancasterian School, New Haven

Schools of Agriculture, &c., &c.
City Trade School, Berlin.
Commercial School, Leghorn.
Agricultural School at Templemoyle.
Institute of Agriculture, Wurtemburg.
School of Arts, Edinburgh.
Polytechnic Institute, Vienna.
Technical School, Zurich
Institute of the Arts, Berlin.
Mechanic Institutions, London.
" " Manchester
Factory Schools.
Adult Schools. Sunday Schools.

Tribute to Gallaudet.—A Discourse in Commemoration of the Life, Character, and Services of the Rev. Thomas H. Gallaudet L L. D., delivered before the citizens of Hartford, January 7th, 1852, with an Appendix. By Henry Barnard, L L. D. Philadelphia: H. Cowperthwait & Co.

The above Discourse was delivered before the citizens of Hartford, and published at their request. The Appendix contains several productions of Mr. Gallaudet, of permanent value, with a History of Institutions for Deaf-mutes, in different countries, and particularly of the American Asylum at Hartford, by the author of the Discourse.

CONTENTS.

PESTALOZZI AND HIS EDUCATIONAL SYSTEM.

PESTALOZZI AND PESTALOZZIANISM:—Memoir, and Educational Principles, Methods, and Influence of John Henry Pestalozzi, and Biographical Sketches of several of his Assistants and Disciples; together with Selections from his Publications. In Two Parts. By HENRY BARNARD, LL.D. New York: F. C. BROWNELL, No. 12, Appleton's Building.

PRICE.—*Part I, in paper covers,* $1 25; *Part II, in paper covers,* $1 25; *Parts I and II, in paper covers,* $2.00; *do., in half calf,* $2.50.

PART I.

LIFE AND EDUCATIONAL SYSTEM OF PESTALOZZI.

PART II.

SELECTIONS FROM THE PUBLICATIONS OF PESTALOZZI.

Educational Biography; or Memoirs of Teachers, Educators, and Promoters and Benefactors of Education, Literature, and Science. By Henry Barnard, LL.D. Part I. *Teachers and Educators.* Vol. I., United States. New York: F. C. Brownell, 413 Broadway. Hartford: F. B. Perkins. *Illustrated Edition:* Price, $3.50, in half Turkish Morocco, or English Calf.

Contents of Volume I.

We are glad to see that Dr. Barnard has consented to let his publishers bring together into one volume, the memoirs of eminent American Teachers and Educators which have appeared in the first series of the *American Journal of Education.* Richly bound, and illustrated with over twenty Portraits, from engravings on steel or copper by our best artists, it is the most creditable tribute which has yet been paid in English Literature to the scholastic profession. It forms a splendid and appropriate gift-book to Teachers, and Promoters of Educational Improvement.—*Connecticut Common School Journal. for February,* 1859.

This elegant and useful contribution to educational literature will, we trust, receive a cordial welcome from teachers. Nothing ever issued from the press could be a more appropriate ornament for the teacher's library or center-table.—*Massachusetts Teacher, for February,* 1859.

GERMAN UNIVERSITIES.

THE GERMAN UNIVERSITIES. Being the fourth volume of the *History of Education.* By KARL VON RAUMER. Re-published from the "*American Journal of Education,*" edited by HENRY BARNARD. LL.D. New York: F. C. BROWNELL, No. 346, Broadway. 250 pages. Price $1.50.

CONTENTS.

PAPERS

For The Teacher.

Number Two—1860.

CONTENTS.

OBJECT TEACHING AND ORAL LESSONS ON SOCIAL SCIENCE AND COMMON THINGS, WITH VARIOUS ILLUSTRATIONS OF THE PRINCIPLES AND PRACTICE OF PRIMARY EDUCATION, AS ADOPTED IN THE MODEL AND TRAINING SCHOOLS OF GREAT BRITAIN.

Published and for sale by

F. C. BROWNELL, 25 HOWARD STREET, NEW YORK.

GEORGE SHERWOOD, LAKE STREET, CHICAGO.

PRICE, $1.50 bound in cloth.

PAPERS

For The Teacher.

Number Four.

CONTENTS.

EDUCATIONAL APHORISMS AND SUGGESTIONS, ANCIENT AND MODERN.

Published and for sale by

F. C. BROWNELL, 25 HOWARD STREET, NEW YORK.

GEORGE SHERWOOD, 124 LAKE STREET, CHICAGO.

PRICE, $1.50 bound in cloth.

THE AMERICAN JOURNAL OF EDUCATION.

EDITED BY HENRY BARNARD, LL. D.

FIRST SERIES. FIVE VOLUMES.

THE FIRST SERIES of Barnard's American Journal of Education consists of five volumes, each volume having an average of 800 pages, embellished with at least four portraits from engravings on steel, of eminent teachers, educators, and promoters of education, and with a large number of wood-cuts, illustrative of recent improvements in the structure, furniture, and arrangements of buildings designed for educational uses.

The series, uniformly and neatly bound, with an index to each volume, and a general index to the whole, will be delivered to the order of subscribers, and forwarded by express, or otherwise, as may be directed, at the expense of the subscriber, on the following

TERMS: For the entire series, in seventeen parts or numbers,						$10.50.
"	"	"	in five volumes, bound in paper covers,			11.25.
"	"	"	"	"	bound in cloth,	12.50.
"	"	"	"	"	bound in leather,	15,00.

THE FIRST SERIES will be found to contain important contributions to,—

1. A HISTORY OF EDUCATION, ancient and modern.
2. ORGANIZATION, ADMINISTRATION, AND SUPPORT OF PUBLIC INSTRUCTION.
3. ELEMENTARY INSTRUCTION IN THE PRINCIPAL COUNTRIES OF EUROPE.
4. NATIONAL EDUCATION IN THE UNITED STATES; or contributions to the history and improvement of common or public schools, and other institutions, means and agencies of popular education in the several states.
5. SCHOOL ARCHITECTURE: or the principles of construction, ventilation, warming, acoustics, seating, &c., applied to school rooms, lecture halls, and class rooms, with illustrations.
6. NORMAL SCHOOLS, and other institutions, means, and agencies for the professional training and improvement of teachers.
7. SYSTEM OF PUBLIC EDUCATION FOR LARGE CITIES AND VILLAGES; with an account of the schools and other means of popular education and recreation in the principal cities of Europe and in this country.
8. SYSTEM OF POPULAR EDUCATION FOR SPARSEDLY POPULATED DISTRICTS.
9. SCHOOLS OF AGRICULTURE, and other means of advancing agricultural improvement.
10. SCHOOLS OF SCIENCE, applied to the mechanic arts, civil engineering, &c.
11. SCHOOLS OF TRADE, NAVIGATION, COMMERCE, &C.
12. FEMALE EDUCATION; with an account of the best seminaries for females in this country and in Europe.
13. INSTITUTIONS FOR ORPHANS.
14. SCHOOLS OF INDUSTRY; or institutions for truant, idle, or neglected children, before they have been convicted of crime.
15. REFORM SCHOOLS: or institutions for young criminals.
16. HOUSES OF REFUGE, for adult criminals.
17. SECONDARY EDUCATION: including 1. institutions preparatory to college, and 2. institutions preparatory to special schools of agriculture, engineering, trade, navigation, &c.
18. COLLEGES AND UNIVERSITIES.
19. SCHOOLS OF THEOLOGY, LAW, AND MEDICINE.
20. MILITARY AND NAVAL SCHOOLS.
21. SUPPLEMENTARY EDUCATION; including adult schools, evening schools, courses of popular lectures debating classes, mechanic institutes, &c.
22. LIBRARIES; with hints for the purchase, arrangement, catalogueing, drawing and preservation of books, especially in libraries designed for popular use.
23. INSTITUTIONS FOR THE DEAF AND DUMB, BLIND, AND IDIOTS.
24. SOCIETIES FOR THE ENCOURAGEMENT OF SCIENCE, THE ARTS, AND EDUCATION.
25. PUBLIC MUSEUMS AND GALLERIES.
26. PUBLIC GARDENS, and other sources of popular recreation.
27. EDUCATIONAL TRACTS; or a series of short essays on topics of immediate practical importance to teachers and school officers.
28. EDUCATIONAL BIOGRAPHY; or the lives of distinguished educators and teachers.
29. EDUCATIONAL BENEFACTORS; or an account of the founders and benefactors of educational and scientific institutio .
30. SELF-EDUCATION; or hints for self formation, with examples of the pursuit of knowledge under difficulties.
31. HOME EDUCATION; with illustrations drawn from the Family Training of different countries.
32. A CATALOGUE of the best publications on the organization, instruction, and discipline of schools, of every grade, and on the principles of education, in the English, French, and German languages.
33. EDUCATIONAL NOMENCLATURE AND INDEX; or an explanation of words and terms used in describing the systems and institutions of education in different countries, with reference to the books where the subjects are discussed and treated of.

BARNARD'S AMERICAN JOURNAL OF EDUCATION.

THE following circular is addressed in answer to numerous inquiries on one or more of the points briefly treated of.

REGULAR SUBSCRIBERS. The terms to regular subscribers are $4 for the year, or for two volumes, or for four consecutive numbers. To non-subscribers the charge is $1.50 per number, and $3 for a single volume.

SPECIMEN NUMBERS. To persons applying for specimen numbers of *Barnard's American Journal of Education*, with a view of becoming subscribers, a copy of the last number issued will be mailed, on receipt of seventy-five cents, half the price at which single numbers are sold, and twelve cents in stamps for prepayment of postage, at the office of publication.

POSTAGE. The law applicable to postage on this quarterly periodical is as follows: "For each periodical, not exceeding three ounces in weight, to any part of the United States, one cent; for every additional ounce or fraction of an ounce, one cent. If paid quarterly or yearly in advance, at the office where the same is either mailed or delivered, then half the above rates are charged." The weight of each number of this Journal is from thirteen to seventeen ounces; making full postage from eleven to fifteen cents per number, or from forty-four to sixty cents a year; and postage paid in advance, at either end of the route, six to eight cents per number, or from twenty-two to thirty cents a year.

MAILING. The numbers of the Journal—done up in single wrapper of stout post-office paper, and, when addressed beyond New England and New York, tied up with strong twine—are mailed to the post-office address of each subscriber who has paid up his subscription for the year, on or before the day of publication of each number, viz., the 15th of March, June, September, and December. If a number does not reach its destination in due time, the fault is not with this office.

EXCHANGES. The publisher looks for the usual courtesy of a notice of the reception, and a specification at least of the *subjects of the several articles*, from those journals which have solicited an exchange, and an omission of this courtesy is supposed to indicate that no further exchange is desired.

THE FIRST SERIES. A general index (*sixty-four pages, nonpareil, double columns,*) of the topics treated of in the first five volumes of the Journal, will be sent, free of expense, to the address of any person making application for the same.

BOUND VOLUMES. Volumes I. II. III. IV. V. VI. VII. VIII. and succeeding volumes when completed, will be furnished, neatly and uniformly bound in cloth with an Index to each volume, and a General Index to each five volumes, at $3.00 for single volume, and $2.50, for two or more volumes.

MEMOIR OF PESTALOZZI, RAUMER'S GERMAN UNIVERSITIES, AND PAPERS FOR THE TEACHER. Subscribers and purchasers of complete sets of the *American Journal of Education* are advised, that nearly all of the contents of these separate works have been, or will be, embraced as articles in the Journal; and that, unless they wish to have them in a compact and convenient form, they need not purchase them.

FREDERIC B. PERKINS,

Publisher of Barnard's American Journal of Education.

Hartford, Conn., 1860.

www.ingramcontent.com/pod-product-compliance
Lightning Source LLC
LaVergne TN
LVHW021406110826
845150LV00007B/1808

* 9 7 8 1 4 2 5 5 1 2 1 4 9 *